EURIPIDES'

I0422277

HIPPOLYTUS

A Complete Translation for Students of Classical Studies and
Drama

By

Hilary J. Deighton

PublishNation
www.publishnation.co.uk

Other works by Hilary J. Deighton

The 'Weather-God' in Hittite Anatolia: An Examination of the Archaeological and Textual Sources

A Day in the Life of Ancient Rome

A Day in the Life of Ancient Athens

For the team - Gill, Ruth and Sally
Colleagues, Friends, Classicists

And for Simon – a wonderful student and even better friend

CONTENTS

PREFACE

You are reading this because you know the significance of Greek drama for not just specialist scholars and students, but for the culture of the world. The time of gift and genius that sparked out of a group of fractious city states in a corner of South-Eastern Europe marked by mountains and islands has had an impact on almost every area of study imaginable, and the development of European drama depends upon it. In particular, scholars, students, actors and audiences owe a debt to three great and extraordinary men who lived in the 5th. Century B.C. in the major city of a state that was about the size of Dorset with a population of maybe 150,000: Aischylos (Aeschylus), Sophokles (Sophocles) and Euripides (comes out the same in Latin). They were not the only dramatists in Athens, and we can only mourn the loss of the work of their rivals and hope that more papyri may yet be found in untouched corners to bring more than the odd quotation back to us. They were, however, the three whose extraordinary gifts created drama that has not lost an iota of its power over two and a half thousand years.

Drama began in the sixth century B.C. when one person stepped out from the chorus and began a dialogue with it, becoming the first actor (*protagonist* - there can be only one protagonist). The mighty Aischylos, master of intoxicatingly gorgeous language, introduced the second actor (*deuteragonist*) and from there on in there was drama. The wise and humane Sophokles is credited with the introduction of the third character (*tritagonist*) and developments in scenery, as well as much else, the unsettling Euripides brought drama closer to the world of the ordinary person. There is a reason why theirs are the works that have survived against some pretty steep odds (the burning of the great Library at Alexandria is one of the greatest crimes against culture ever committed. Thank you, Rome.). It may be a safe bet that each of them has a work being produced somewhere every single year - it is not a bet at all that they are being studied in schools, universities, drama schools and homes every single year.

It is important to remember that drama for the Greeks was a part of the rites of Dionysos, part of the civic religious round and civic duty. It was only performed in Athens at two festivals in the year, one in winter and one in early spring. For the main Dionysia in March, three dramatists were chosen to present tragedies (a better translation would be 'serious drama', as not every Greek tragedy has an unhappy ending). The poet, for such he must be, would need to have three tragedies and one satyr play - a piece of cheery bawdiness - for his day, i.e. this was a very different experience of drama. Three plays, which did not have to be and usually were not trilogies, of strong, emotion-wrenching drama were performed one after the other over the day to an audience sitting at first on a hillside, later wooden benches and then stone seating, with their snacks and wineskins and awareness of festival. It is no wonder that they needed the satyr play to release everything that they had lived through on that day. After the tragedians had had their three days the last day was given over to the writers of comedy, the prizes were awarded (more substantial to the citizen who had had to fund the productions than to the creators) - and then that was it till next winter. Drama was powerful, special, it happened in a religious context and only twice a year: imagine the investment required on the part of not just poet and performers, but audiences as well.

If the experience of theatre-going was vastly different then and now, the genius of what was presented shines through against changing times and cultures. Even in their own day the three great dramatic poets' reputations spread across their world. We know the names of some of their competitors (and friends), and can assume that they will have created works we would enjoy, but only fragments remain, alas. Perhaps we should not entirely give up hope that more may yet appear – in my own lifetime our knowledge of the comic playwright Menander has gone from the odd fragment to a selection of entire plays, because of the discovery of well-preserved papyrus scrolls in Egypt. We know there are places where unread papyrus still exists, possibly in a salvageable condition, so important rediscoveries may one day be made. In the meanwhile we find endless satisfaction and interest in the works the Greeks themselves singled out as special.

The difference in attitudes as well as literary style amongst the three greats was so familiar to the Athenian audiences that it could form the basis of a comic play by Aristophanes (*The Frogs*, still funny). Imagine a modern audience finding the humour in the contrast of style and mood of say, Beckett, Shaw and Rattigan to look at a single century, or Shakespeare, Sheridan and Osborne to contrast language and style.

In bringing a new literal translation of *Hippolytos* to the student of Classics or Drama I have used the Oxford text and have included the problematic passage which appears to imply the reappearance of the second chorus which other translations often omit. Students and scholars of Greek will expect to read the entire text and everyone else should have the opportunity to do so as well. It can be omitted in performance if necessary.

Transliteration from Greek causes all sorts of problems, given that for a couple of thousand years there has been an almost universal use of the Latinised versions, and those of us having to decide how to transliterate will at times find it necessary to make some compromises for the sake of ease of use and comprehensibility for those not studying the language. My compromise in this book is to transliterate as strictly as possible, but I have maintained the convention of rendering the short Greek *u* as *y* (the capital in the Greek alphabet is *Y*), not least because it would render the very title of the play perhaps a little too alien for prospective readers and user. The Latinised versions are given in the Guide to Names and Places. The only place in this book on which you will see the Latinised *Hippolytus* is the cover, and that is only because - deeply to my regret - that is the form with which most students and other seekers will be more familiar. Elsewhere, I stick to my principles.

There will be some repetition of information in the following sections, as each can be used as a stand-alone aide depending on the user's purposes.

On the matter of further reading - many of you will be students and therefore should be paying due attention to the preferred reading lists provided by your teachers and lecturers. Look along the library shelves for yourselves (not just superficial computer search engines, please) and read as widely as you can. I shall here recommend only two fundamental works and you can head outward from there: firstly, H.D.F. Kitto's magisterial *Greek Tragedy*, which has for good reasons long been the friend of student and teacher alike, and secondly, Erika Simon's *The Ancient Theatre*, a short but scholarly and comprehensive guide to production in Greek and Roman Theatre.

H.J.D.

INTRODUCTION

Euripides lived from c.485 – 406 B.C. (we can be more sure about the date of death than birth). His family had an ancestral priesthood of Apollo Zosterios, so he must have been of at least respectable birth, even though Aristophanes says his mother was a greengrocer – it may just be a joke about family property on the island of Salamis. It was said he was born on the day of the great Battle of Salamis when Athens defeated mighty Persia (this battle is widely understood to be one of the great pivotal moments of history). This hereditary priesthood – such things ran in families or with particular offices in the Greek world and are not vocation as priesthood is understood today - does not stop Euripides attacking Apollo (for whom read Delphi: the oracle was regularly all about politics and pro-Sparta, and many of the intellectuals of the Athenian Enlightenment were particularly sceptical about oracles) in many of his plays. He was actually challenged to an *antidosis*, i.e. asking another to perform your liturgy (the undertaking by an individual of some expensive service to the state, such as equipping a warship or acting as a *choregos*, funding a production in the drama contests or even more expensively, the choral ones, that avoided the indelicacy of actual taxation for Athenian citizens) or exchange properties - so he must have been considerably more well-off than a greengrocer's son. Supposedly he liked to retire to a cave on Salamis to write. He did not take a prominent part in politics which was the responsibility, as was the army, of every citizen, but he did his bit. He went on an embassy to Syracuse. He was very much part of the intellectual movement of the late 5th. century - tradition has him friends with the philosophers Anaxagoras and Sokrates, amongst others. It is said he was prosecuted for impiety by the thuggish politician, Kleon. It is vital to remember that impiety is a serious matter and seen as an assault on the communal whole - the gods are not disposed to differentiate between individual and community if offended. It was an impiety charge that did for Sokrates, for all the political motivation and inconvenient friends that lay behind the bringing of the charge. All this informs the background of *Hippolytos*.

Euripides wrote many plays (92) and more survive than from any other dramatist (one, *Rhesos*, is no longer considered to be by him). He had little success at the festivals themselves in his lifetime, however. Two of his four victories were posthumous: *Bacchai* and *Iphigeneia in Aulis*. Some of his work got him into trouble - *The Women of Troy* went down very badly, produced just before the launching of the Sicilian expedition (which ended in disaster for Athens but was hyped to the skies in advance) and the year after Melos (which was a disaster for Melos – the Athenians took a vicious revenge on them for seceding from what had become the Athenian Empire and Euripides' play was a nasty reminder of what happens to the victims when a state falls). His first version of the Hippolytos story, in which Phaidra willingly set out to seduce, was hugely unpopular and something of a scandal. The dramatic poet was supposed to support traditional virtues and leave an Athenian audience feeling good about their society – Euripides did not do that and people tend to react rather badly to being made to face unpalatable things.

Famously, Euripides was ill-humoured (possibly just because he liked his own company in a gregarious society, but maybe he really was) and considered in his day thoroughly misogynistic - except in bed, as the joke went. In fact his plays consistently present strong, interesting women whom his audiences were compelled to confront on the same terms as men - very disconcerting for the Athenian male. Some of this woman-hating reputation may indeed stem from the earlier,

6

lost *Hippolytos* and its shameless Phaidra. His compassion for women is remarkable - but no-one gets away easily in Euripides. He has a clear, and not at all comfortable, vision of humanity and human weakness.

For all the gossip about how much he made people uncomfortable, time after time Euripides was indeed one of the three chosen poets. Facts and legends do not always tell identical stories. Euripides left Athens, however, when he was over 70, and went to live in Macedonia. Legend has it he died by being torn to death by the king's hunting dogs - not accepted by many authorities, though some concede it is possible as a ghastly accident. Anyone who has had to shin up a six-foot wall at speed does know that the dogs on Greek farms can still be large and decidedly intimidating (even Odysseus was wary of the farm dogs when he got home to Ithaka). We do know for sure that Euripides did die in Macedonia. Various plays were found in his effects and two produced (possibly finished) either by his son or his nephew. When Sophokles - even older - heard of Euripides' death, he dressed his chorus in mourning. Euripides' plays soon attained the popularity they have never lost.

In terms of lasting influence and popularity, the story of Phaidra and Hippolytos has certainly spoken to playwrights and other artists throughout history. There is, of course, power in the story at its simplest, soap opera level, with forbidden love and rush to vengeance. There is value in considering differing treatments across the centuries - Seneca, Racine and the film maker Jules Dassin are just some of those who have been drawn to this story of unhappy families. The tale has also been tackled in ballet and in music. In this exercise, however, it is important to consider how much a fuller understanding of the religious and cultural context driving these memorable characters adds to the full dramatic wallop. Productions keeping these elements in mind can certainly raise the hairs on the back of the neck.

Euripides has been accused of a range of faults, from atheism to inability to control the structure of his drama, but this usually reflects a lack of understanding of what he is actually trying to do both in terms of presenting a message and devising a drama. As Kitto has pointed out, Euripides presents not so much a drama of character like Sophokles', but a drama of scenes. Certain kinds of scene reappear regularly - recognitions, confrontations, debates or justifications couched virtually in court terms - sometimes the language does not just recall but actually *is* the language of the courtroom. It may be worth considering in this case whether Hippolytos' courtroom-ready 'look at me, I'm wonderful' speech was ever going to be the best way to speak to a father wild with grief and rage, and also to bear in mind that Athenian juries did not stop for sober consideration but acquitted or condemned on the spot, all too easily on the basis of perceived character rather than actual evidence - and did at times have to regret at leisure.

Euripides was an intellectual with a mind formed by rhetoric, enquiry, new science, new ways of looking at the world, a refusal to look for easy answers, or necessarily to expect any answers. He does, in fact, proceed from a profoundly religious understanding, but this provides no comfort. He never criticizes Zeus, in this way expressing a move towards a monotheistic expression of religious understanding to be found in some of the philosophers of the latter part of the 5th. century, most famously Sokrates. He does not, however, write off the other gods as empty myth. Throughout Greek literature the gods are on the one hand held in awe and respect and on the other criticized or even ridiculed (it is worth remembering that God can be funny, though not a figure of ridicule, in Mediaeval mystery plays). In plays like *Hippolytos* or the *Bacchai*, the gods personify for Euripides, as they would for many of his peers and in other cultures, powerful forces which cannot be denied. The latter play is one of the most terrifying ever written about the perils of attempting to bypass the demands of religion.

Of all Euripides' plays, *Hippolytos* above all is the one hardest for an audience to view in our day without seeing it through a curtain of Freud. Aphrodite and Artemis are monsters from the Id (to quote *Forbidden Planet*) but - and this is a vital but - they are also divine creatures terrible in their demands, implacable in their machinations and ultimately rather feeble in responding even to those humans who best try to serve them. We dare not judge them by human standards, their agendas and realities are not ours. It is a disservice to Euripides for modern productions to fail to understand the deep religious understanding that impels the narrative, as they all too often now do. The gods, the forces of otherness, the drives that lie beyond surface and mundane, they are dangerous because they actually, really matter. To reduce Hippolytos and Phaidra only to slaves of their own human weaknesses is to traduce Euripides and to diminish ourselves. The fact that the personifications of the gods do not always seem exactly admirable is neither here nor there to the actuality of their power and influence. The idea of a consistent, just, merciful God with an intimate concern for each and every person who is able to be approached at a deep level through e.g. contemplative prayer is one which most people in the ancient world would not have comprehended. Theirs was for the most part a religion of observance, careful, precise and vital, rather than personal relationship, and the fear of the grim consequences for non-observance was very real. This is at the heart of *Hippolytos*, but it is not a freak thing confined to drama, it pervaded the ancient world. The reason the penalty for a Vestal Virgin in Rome losing her qualification (only enforced during her time of office, this was not a lifetime commitment) was so deliberately dreadful - burial alive, conveyed to her tomb in shocking silence - was that her fall from grace was genuinely perceived as an awful act of blasphemy threatening the safety and well-being of the whole state. *Hippolytos* is not just a play about three people with character flaws, it is about the big stuff.

One further general attitude of the Greek world that modern audiences may not always give full weight is the pressures and demands of a Heroic culture - and the Classical world retained the ethos of a Heroic culture even in the most developed and sophisticated cities. The essence is summed up as the difference between 'shame' cultures and 'guilt' cultures. They lived in the former, we live in the latter. To oversimplify: in a shame culture, the sense of having done wrong and the problem of living with it is really imposed from without. In fifth century Greek there was no word for sin – the one used in the New Testament originally meant the arrow missing the mark. Most cultures regard stealing from neighbours and killing one's granny as bad things, but in the ancient Greek world stealing from one's enemies and killing or enslaving their grannies was perfectly all right. There was no sense of moral guides and rules which apply to everyone and from which one could know oneself to be falling away and hence to feel guilt at transgression. The gods were not the moral arbiters - if they were not watching, or not interested, then one got away with it. As there was no concept of sin, as we understand it, there was, crucially, no concept of the possibility of repentance and the comfort of forgiveness either. There was also none of the much more modern concept of forgiving oneself, whether a wise guidance to the troubled or an easy excuse for the morally lazy. There is nowhere to hide. When honour is lost, it is public, inescapable, unforgiven. Heroic cultures are not unique to the distant past or faraway cultures: Japanese bushido, Mediaeval chivalry, Prussian military honour are all examples, and if these do not help, think Klingon. The characters in drama live and die at a heightened level, but according to rules which the original audience fully understood.

Hippolytos, produced in 428, is one of the very few Euripidean dramas that actually won a prize. It is a good read, but really gripping on stage. His earlier version, with Phaidra complicit in her guilty lust, was a resounding flop. Possibly Euripides himself was dissatisfied with a treatment that let the woman take the blame, and perhaps it lacked the tensions that make the second version a true tragedy. Maybe it was just not all that good – even a genius can have an off-day, and we do not have the day's other two offerings to judge.

There is no surprise in the story. Aphrodite appears at the beginning - it is very unusual for a god to appear at the beginning of a play - and tells us exactly what is going to happen. We can then shiver in dismay as we watch it. Phaidra, Hippolytos, and to an extent Theseus, are three lives out of kilter in response to Aphrodite. Phaidra is a good woman caught in a desperate struggle against an unwanted desire, Hippolytos will not allow of desire, Theseus is carried away by jealousy. His reaction, though high-handed, is not as far from reason as the other two, the one through no fault of her own, the other through a fatal single-mindedness. Hippolytos must learn that a god must not be set at nothing, elemental forces cannot be denied, and unfortunately for them, innocent bystanders will get hurt in the process of that learning. That, to Aphrodite, is neither here nor there. She must punish Hippolytos for presuming to turn his back on her. His patroness, Artemis, can only offer him at the end the unlikely comfort that she will get payback from one of Aphrodite's favourites. She will not even stick around to see her favourite die – that would be a pollution, and he appears to understand that, although his final words to her could be seen as having an ambiguity. The mortals do not get compassion from the gods, but the gods must not be resisted or ignored. They must have due honour.

Euripides uses the goddesses to frame the action very deliberately. This is a tragedy of victims, not those who act. Poor Phaidra does attempt to be an actor, and it is her struggle against the power of Aphrodite's imposed desire that makes her one of the most interesting and moving of all female characters in Greek drama. For the Greeks, the very irrationality of desire - it arrives without warning or reason and can make a fool of the strongest of us - was very much seen as something imposed externally: some god must have made me do it; Eros made me mad with love. This is expressed in Eros' arrows - they pierce you from without. The Greeks both accepted *and* suspected this attitude; it is, after all, such a convenient excuse. Euripides accepts the external power, Aphrodite, as a power of nature. Sexual desire is necessary if life is to exist, but it can also be terrifying - the chorus prays not to be caught by its extremes.

Euripides does, however, also see the enemy within. Phaidra remembers her own fatal heritage of unnatural desire, and there is a sense of evil waiting in the blood, in the genes as we would now say, and this sense also informs Euripides' work in this and other plays. So we humans can be the target of forces from without, or attacked from the old *hamartia*, the fatal flaw in the character of the otherwise great man - a key ingredient in tragedy - within. Although Phaidra is mostly just the unlucky instrument of Aphrodite's plan, she does also carry an old taint - and bad blood will always out in Greek drama.

Like many Euripidean women, however, Phaidra seeks to preserve her honour just as a man would. She wants to preserve herself from doing something dreadful, she wants to preserve her good name (*very* important to the Greek mind), she wants to preserve the honour of her family.

Both Phaidra and Hippolytos, the one from necessity, the other by chance, fail to uphold the traditional aristocratic virtue of *sophrosyne*: sensible, self-controlled living (for Sophokles so important as the necessary balance which must be restored when tragic events throw life out of kilter). Phaidra loses it through her cruel passion, cruelly imposed, but then in order to protect her name she takes a cruel vengeance on Hippolytos in the letter.

Hippolytos likes to think of himself as the embodiment of *sophrosyne*, but his rejection - contemptuous rejection - of Aphrodite shows this to be *hubris*. This is one of those useful Greek words that needs to be translated by a paragraph, which is why it has passed unchanged into English usage. In brief, it means going beyond what the gods allow - getting above yourself, forgetting your place. It provokes *nemesis*, i.e. the gods' righteous indignation, which is a very bad idea because it is followed by *ate*, ruin. Remember: whom the gods wish to destroy they first make mad (the tipping point when the *hamartia*, the fatal flaw, drives him too far). This can happen to the greatest of men and in fact for Aristotle the essence of tragedy is the suffering of the greatest of men – for the Greeks there is no working through of emotion to bring cleansing (*catharsis*) by watching the little guy get stomped on by fate. Tragedy lies in watching the great fall into ghastly traps of their own making. In Hippolytos' case he lacks the two basic qualities necessary to *sophrosyne*: insight into one's own nature (*gnothi seauton* = know yourself, very important to Greek thought, and carved on the Temple of Apollo at Delphi) and avoidance of extremes (*meden agan* = nothing too much, also vital to Greek thought). Until his imminent demise forces some emotional growth onto him, Hippolytos is a self-satisfied prig whose neurotic rejection of the power of sex and of women as a species not only does insult to the goddess but also offends against the norms of his society. In our society celibacy is an available and not necessarily remarkable choice (despite the impression of advertising and media). In Ancient Greece, there might be brief periods of ritual abstinence for particular festivals or purification, but celibacy as a chosen lifestyle did not exist. Men would have sex with anything on legs, women would marry - to reject this is to stand outside society, and he who stands outside society will usually be cut down.

(Just as a side and necessarily too brief issue, no-one would have raised a passing eyebrow if Hippolytos had had an eye for his hunting chums. Bisexuality was an unremarkable thing for men in the ancient world, the distinction being rather between active and passive partner, but exclusive homosexuality in a grown-up was not well-regarded by Athenians because one must, above all, protect and further the family line. Hippolytos could dislike women till the cows came home so long as he had sex with one of appropriate status in order to produce sons, and respected Aphrodite's power over this essential drive. His prudery is a social and religious flaw, his disrespect is fatal.)

A political dimension to Hippolytos' downfall has been suggested: Hippolytos claims for himself a characteristically aristocratic virtue, and he is a huntsman, a characteristically aristocratic pastime (well, up to a point, Lord Copper). He is certainly pretty snooty, but the point is really not to do with his standing with men but his standing with the gods. One cannot refuse to give a god due honour. Aphrodite does not mind that he is a devotee of Artemis, he is quite free to be - his mistake is in slighting her. In this Euripides seems to agree with the other great poets of drama: man cannot deny or defy the power of forces that lie beyond man. While one should not deny Euripides a religious outlook - he is *not* an atheist - he would surely have combined some of his treatment of these issues with psychological technical vocabulary had he had it available to him (and it is no accident at all that psychological technical vocabulary we use today is heavily dependent, as are most 'ologies', on Greek). Religion and psychological insight are not in opposition today and, as we have touched on, it diminishes Euripides to suggest he could only fall into one camp in his time. The Greeks had a sharp understanding of the works of the mind, and if you do not have scientific vocabulary available, you can present truth very efficiently in a story. That is worth bearing in mind in a range of contexts.

Hippolytos' determined rejection of sex, not for passing matters of purity or an intellectual exercise, makes him look like a weirdo - his father reckons he has fallen under the sway of cults, accusing him of being part of an Orphic cult and a vegetarian (not so long ago that would be enough to mark you out as worryingly odd in our society), which actually in the Greek world really was to set yourself apart from the norms of society - it meant you would not partake in the feasts after sacrifice, you were not part of the community. But then Hippolytos is also a hunter and a devotee of the huntress goddess. Theseus (who put it about a bit, and raped Hippolytos' mother, the Amazon Hippolyta, but that is how heroes behave in his world) is just trying to get a handle on his peculiar son. Another recent suggestion is that Hippolytos' rejection of sex may be a memory of hunting magic.

It has been suggested that Hippolytos can be seen as a rare male example of a person stuck at the periphery of life, with his rites of passage into full adulthood never to be completed. He is a Lost Boy. Artemis represents the time out of normality when virgin girls are separated from society before marriage, when they will be reintegrated. She is ever-virgin, an option not open to a human girl (who might well be on the threshold of the unknown far more than any modern Western bride) and who might wish to stay on one side of the threshold because that is familiarity, childhood, safety - but the girl must pass through into sexuality, into the norms of society. In many cultures, rites of passage still include seclusion or time spent in the wild before reintegration and a recognition of sexual development, ready for adulthood and marriage.

Hippolytos is stuck on the edge - but as a mortal he cannot be stuck on the edge. Actually he is stuck on the edge in another way - he is illegitimate. On both those counts, virginity and illegitimacy, he is marginal to society. He is also a member of a royal family – one that implodes. It is not an uncommon element in tragedy to see the pitiful and fearful downfall of an ancient house, which is cathartic not only to the emotions but to the *polis* (the city or state and its embodiment as a community), as it clears the way for a new foundation.

It is good for the community that the odd one out dies, but the tragedy can also end with the promise of the growth of a cult - both a tying-in of past and present (there would be reference to actual known cults at the time the play was written) and a kind of tying of the oddness back into the community.

A certain irony lies in the fact that, while Hippolytos is actually off-balance in the way he rants against women, it is a woman who causes the tragedy to fall in on our characters - but it is not Phaidra, it is the Nurse. There is a range of views on the Nurse: whether she is a wicked old procuress, a loving nurse just trying to do the best to help her charge, or simply a practical peasant-woman looking for an answer, and how she is interpreted is a particularly interesting point for staging the drama. Telling Hippolytos certainly *is* an answer, just a really bad one. She does also hint at magic, which is women's domain.

In fact hers is the first mistake in not a comedy, but a tragedy of errors. Everyone misunderstands everyone else, until at the end the *dea ex machina* (literally - it means the goddess on the crane, and that could be how the gods would appear in Greek drama, hoisted above the human action) arrives to explain things and give some pointers to the future (e.g. the cult that will be set up). This is a device Euripides uses quite regularly, sometimes when he has actually finished examining what he was interested in examining in dramatic terms, and now just has to get the *i*s dotted and the *t*s crossed, like Hercule Poirot rounding off an Agatha Christie. Here, however, Artemis is very strongly to the point. She has been Hippolytos' one devotion, she is the antithesis of Aphrodite, she is out to get her own back - not actually on Aphrodite herself, of course, but some other poor wretch of an innocent victim. She cannot shed a tear for her favourite, and will not even stay to watch him die. The gods have their own agenda, the forces they embody do not give concessions to the frailty of humanity. Of course Aphrodite's power should not be gainsaid - the denial of sexuality is ultimately the denial of life, though more immediately for a Greek understanding, the denial of community. Hippolytos is never integrated into life.

He is at least reintegrated into his family at the end. Like Sidney Carton, nothing in life becomes him like the leaving of it. All the compassion and forgiveness he has hitherto denied (certainly denied any woman) is now poured out, and he comforts his father and releases him from pollution and any curse that might fall on him for the shedding of innocent blood. He is the only one who actually does any forgiving: Aphrodite does not forgive and destroys several lives in the process, Phaidra in the end takes vengeance on Hippolytos to protect her own honour, Theseus takes vengeance on Hippolytos for his imagined crime (note how quick Theseus is to believe every word), Artemis is going to take vengeance on Aphrodite, via a helpless human. Hippolytos forgives his father - transforming our perceptions of him as he does so.

A source of scandal in the ancient world was Hippolytos' angry statement to the Nurse that his tongue swore but his mind did not. This should cause a sharp intake of breath - oaths were of enormous importance to the Greeks, and under the

17

supervision of Zeus. It is quite a significant point in Euripides' slightly earlier *Medeia* that the Greeks, who were supposed to be so hot on oaths, actually broke their word, while the barbarians kept theirs. Here, in fact, the scandalising phrase is taken out of context. Hippolytos actually gets cursed by his father precisely because he *does* keep his oath and does not betray Phaidra's story, so he does do the decent thing, and once more Euripides is wilfully misunderstood for making people consider uncomfortable truths.

Over his career, Euripides moved away from the chorus as the integral character of its origins - remember that drama originates when one actor steps out from it and starts to interact with the rest. Compare his later works with Aischylos and the contrast will be very clear. Sometimes his chorus seems almost an embarrassment, although it can also serve its traditional function of drawing us in and forcing us to confront our perceptions of the action. Sometimes, as indeed here, he seems to dangle in front of us the possibility that if the chorus just spoke up it could change the outcome of the action, e.g. in telling Theseus what it knows. This would contravene the rules of drama because the chorus is supposed to comment and reflect on the action, not take part in it, but Euripides was an innovator, pushing drama in new directions in terms of dramatic structure, production design and music - partly, of course, why he was so unpopular in some quarters in his day, quite apart from his unsettling perceptions of the human condition and determination to rub Athenian noses in things they would rather avoid, like the treatment of the victims of war or the position of women and the poorer people in society.

For many, however, his big selling point *was* his choruses. Sadly, we have no way to know what the music sounded like (though some reconstructions have been attempted), but we do have the great beauty of the words of his choral passages. These were memorised and sung. The story goes, indeed, that some Athenian prisoners were released from the hellish conditions of the quarries where they were being held after the military disaster in Sicily because they could entertain new Syracusan masters with Euripides. Just as it is too easy to write Euripides off as an atheist, it is also too easy to write off his choruses and suggest he was pushing towards getting rid of them. Against this one could note that in this play there are two choruses, one of which has to leave as soon as it has arrived but may reappear later. There is nothing like this anywhere else in drama and it breaks the rules in a big way. No-one has a good explanation for this and the relevant passage is frequently left out in translations. Euripides has new ideas about what he wants to achieve. The (main) chorus certainly voices a central theme of the play,

"Eros ... never appear to me with evil intent or undue measure!"

GREEK TRAGEDY – A ROUND-UP OF ESSENTIALS

The glories of Greek drama that we still cherish and relish belong to such a small space of time - the one extraordinary century, the 5th. century B.C., when a torchlight seems to have shone out of the heavens on one small, fragmented, belligerent, staggeringly talented corner of Europe which continues to influence the world in countless ways every single day. Fascinating and important things happened both before and after, but this is the century that changes everything. Other cultures had forms of drama, but whether the richness of European drama would have evolved without the genius of the Greeks and their three most celebrated representatives in this art is a question that should provide hours of entertaining debate. The following refers only to tragedy - comedy follows its own rules and will not be dealt with here.

The beginning of drama is religious rite and it continues throughout the Greek world to be part of religious rite, however tenuous that connection might in the end become. Originally, the function of drama as part of religious rite was so important that there was a public fund to enable as many as possible to attend. You did not decide on a night out and go to see what might be playing at your local theatre. Drama in Athens was confined to the Great Dionysia and the Lenaia, festivals of Dionysos. He is a much more powerful and mysterious deity than his commonly known function as god of wine might suggest. In fact the association with wine is more to do with the fact that wine (not to be underestimated because it is after all a staple part of the diet and economy) has a transformative power. Dionysos is actually a disturbing god, because he speaks of otherness, transcendence, wildness, religious ecstasy - man's acceptance that he is not in control. Any facile writing him off as a jolly drunk festooned with bunches of grapes will be soon dispelled by any acquaintance with another of the masterworks of Euripides, the *Bacchai*. This is a good read, but in performance utterly electrifying - and makes good background material for anyone seeking to stage *Hippolytos*. This is not to say that jolly and drunken things did not happen at some of his festivals as well, but always remember that the reality is complex.

Tragedy nowadays is understood to mean something with an unhappy ending. To the Greeks it would have meant simply serious drama and there are extant 'tragedies' with happy endings. A long classroom or rehearsal room debate could be carried on about whether or why the stories that end badly are greater or more powerful (I refer you to Aristotle's *Poetics* and Longinus' *On Sublimity* - essential reading for the aspiring artist in any sphere, or critic). The thing to remember, however, is that in Greek literature tragedy indicates a genre, not necessarily an outcome. Audiences might know the base story, or a version of it, but they would have no idea what the poet was going to do with it and how everything would turn out. There are, for example, versions of the Oidipous (Oedipus) legend in which he lives happily ever after, or different versions of the fate of Medeia's (Medea's) children. It was exceedingly rare for a poet to present a completely invented plot (we only know of one), rather than use at least the basic characters of known stories. Aischylos has left us a rarity in his historical play, *Persai*, an imaging of the impact on the then current Persian emperor, Xerxes, of his recent defeat by the Greeks (especially, of course, the Athenians – Aischylos was prouder of his state and of his military service than his magnificent poetry). Then as now, of course, the dramatist could make his point with allegory, and Euripides could be a very disturbing gadfly, directly challenging the perceptions and prejudices of the audience.

No-one really knows how the word tragedy evolved. The literal meaning of goat-song is not hugely helpful. There was a theory around in antiquity that it might have had something to do with a prize of a goat or a sacrifice of a goat, which would be the expected sacrifice to Dionysos. Satyrs, who are creatures of Dionysos and who appear in the bawdy romps that would round off a day of intense dramas at the festivals, could be half goat, but in Athens satyrs would be half horse, so that does not necessarily help, and it is in Athens that the first vital step takes place - and it is literally a step. At some point in the latter part of the 6th. century B.C., an actor stepped out from a religious chorus and started interacting with it. According to legend, the first actor was Thespis - hence thespian. The tradition of solemn choral dances (the *dithyramb*) continues alongside the development of drama, so the one does not supersede the other.

The first actor is the protagonist (please note for ever after that you can never have more than one first actor so that protagonist should never appear in the plural unless you are discussing more than one work). The mighty Aischylos, the first of the three great masters, introduced the deuteragonist, the second actor, and true drama is born. The wise Sophokles introduced the third actor, the tritagonist, as well as scene painting. Obviously having a third character available on stage allows for new areas of interaction, misunderstanding and tension. According to Greek dramatic convention, there can never be more than three actors with speaking parts on stage, but the gadfly Euripides does at times allow for a fourth non-speaking actor (laying himself open to parody by the comic playwrights, but that unspeaking presence can be telling). Of course, there are more characters, but only three actual people doing all the acting roles. The poet himself could well be one of them. Such restrictions on speaking roles on stage are not confined to Greece - there are similar conventions e.g. with French classical drama. While it may seem odd when described, it will never cross the mind when one is actually caught up in the action. Everyone taking part would, of course, be male. Athens may have been the archetypal radical democracy, but it was actually a very stratified society, designed to protect the interest of the citizens, who were a defined group of men - not women, not resident aliens (Metics), not visitors, not slaves. All citizens were the government and were the army, but they were in the minority of the population. It is not known for sure whether women even got to go to the theatre, although there is an often-quoted reference to the terrifying appearance of the Furies in *The Eumenides* causing miscarriage.

The actors are only a part of the characters of a Greek drama, however. A vital role is played by the chorus and one can easily trace the development of its role through the works of the three great dramatic poets. They are often the first cast members to appear as they dance on, they observe the whole action, and they are often the last to go. They help set the scene, put the action into context, remind us of back story or relevant history/mythology, act as Everyman commenting on and reacting to what they see unfold. The actors address them and interact with them, appeal to them, try to justify themselves to them, but the chorus should not affect the progress of the story. To diminish the importance of the chorus was regarded as a fault in drama, and in terms of the entertainment value their songs and dances were integral to the spectacle. This was all, of course, part of the expense of production, although cheaper than having to fork out for the dithyramb, and part of what caught judges' eyes.

The place of the chorus is the *orchestra* (in Greek and in this context pronounced orchaystra - *ch* as in Scottish loch), the circular dancing floor. The circular shape has led to speculation that drama may have developed out of festivals held on a threshing floor, but we simply do not know. The actors may perform in the orchestra as well as on the stage platform and on occasion roof of the stage building, but the chorus can never go in the other direction. There was an altar in the centre of the orchestra as all drama was part of the rites of Dionysos. There could be some props, although the space largely needed to be clear for dancing.

There would be originally a pool of 50 chorus members, although they were not all used in performance for all four of the plays in a programme. Aischylos divided them into groups of 12 and Sophokles into groups of 15. There would be a chorus leader, and it would be he who would interact in dialogue with the actors, while all would share in the songs and dance. Choral passages are divided into verses, *strophe* and answering *antistrophe* often with a closing verse, *epode*. It has been suggested that the chorus danced in different directions for strophe and antistrophe and faced front for the epode. Singing was unison (harmony was a later development in musical understanding - Plato had an interest in the theory of music), and the usual accompaniment would be a flute - actually more like a recorder or even an oboe - possibly with the addition of strings (a harp, lyre or the more elaborate kithara) and occasionally percussion. There have been attempts to recreate Greek choral music and it is worth seeking out recordings to get a feel for it. Some musical notation has been found, though not for drama.

The actors also sang - long speeches would in fact have been arias. There were also duets. The rapid-fire *stichomythia* interchanges between actors and sometimes chorus which advance the plot like recitative in opera would be spoken. It is therefore helpful to compare Greek tragedy with *singspiel* opera in which one does find arias, duets, ensembles and choruses, with occasional spoken passages. The fusion of song,

24

dance and colour that was the reality stands in quite strong contrast with many people's image of a rather sombre production for Greek drama, although nowadays that can sometimes just come down to the availability of funding. Try putting this together with another culture shock for the unaware: all that gorgeous, serene white marble statuary was actually painted really bright colours. Greece was a vibrant place.

The audience did not know what they were going to see, so they had to be told. This can be done by means of a prologue, with e.g. a watchman waiting for the signal that the fleet is coming home from Troy and musing from his post about where we are and how things stand. Sometimes the chorus comes in first and their entry song will set the scene for us. Someone does actually have to say where we are and with whom we are dealing (this is, of course, not the only dramatic tradition in which this is necessary).

The entry of the chorus is called the *parodos*. It is followed by *episodes*, which are when the actors take over and the plot moves forward. These alternate with *stasima* (singular: *stasimon*), which are the choral passages. These allow the audience to identify with the reactions of the chorus and let the chorus fill in background or context. They can also cover the passage of time although dramas do tend to observe the unities of time, place and action – not only practically a good solution to the physical circumstances of production but also, and primarily, concentrating the tension and emotion. The final scene is the *exodos* in which everything gets wrapped up and the chorus dances off, often having had the last word. (Remember that there are no curtains, it is daylight and the only way for anyone in the orchestra to get on and off is to be seen doing it.) All tragedies conform to this pattern. Laid out as a plan it looks restrictive and even clinical, but in performance one is simply swept along by the story. *Hippolytos* presents a real problem in that there is one chorus for the beginning (Huntsmen) who must then have to make a very hasty retreat in order for the chorus who will be in the orchestra for the duration to dance on (the women of Troizen). There is even a possibility that the Huntsmen were supposed to return midway. There is nothing like this in any other drama and it contravenes the rules completely. It remains a mystery.

The turning point in a story is typically a recognition scene (*anagnorisis*) - this might be the realisation who a character really is e.g. Electra recognising her brother and then the pair of them can move on to the business of murdering Mother, or more often *peripeteia* (pronounced peripet eye a) the characters' recognition that they have got things horribly wrong, everything is reversed from what they had believed and the inexorable consequences cannot now be averted. In *Hippolytos* both Hippolytos himself and Theseus get these 'what have I done?' moments. It is of the essence of tragedy that the *hamartia* becomes inescapably clear to the hero as well as to everyone else, particularly the resentful gods and their *nemesis* (righteous indignation leading to taking action to punish it), and now it is onwards to *ate* (ruin and the steps the unfortunate hero will end up taking, very possibly with a push from the gods, in order to ensure it). In the happier sort of drama *anagnorisis* can mean e.g. a castaway Orestes recognising his long-lost and presumed sacrificed sister Iphigeneia. Poor Oidipous has so many elements of recognition to handle in that most richly and ironically complex of plays that the burden becomes almost as unbearable to watch as to endure. He is the perfect example of *peripeteia* - everything he believed his life to be built on is wrong. For Aristotle, indeed, Oidipous is the touchstone of every level of excellence in drama. Watch out in Greek drama for these important passages where the realisation hits and everything changes for ever.

An interesting footnote to Oidipous is that Sophokles could not have foreseen one last great irony for his endlessly fascinating masterpiece. The original Greek name is *Oidipous the Tyrant* (students will see this referred to regularly by the familiar academic shorthand of *O.T.* not *O.R.*). Tyrant is not a pejorative term in Greek but the technical term for a self-made or appointed ruler, which is what Oidipous believes himself to be. The Latin name and its translation, *Oedipus Rex*, i.e. Oedipus the King, give the game away from the start because one of the greatest and most painful ironies is that he is, in fact, the rightful king. The point of this is that there are lessons here about always going back to the original source and not making cultural assumptions. Sticking with Sophokles and the Theban plays we can also cite the frequent modern misrepresentation of Antigone as a freedom fighter, which misses what for Sophokles was the whole point of the play, i.e. the trans-cendence of religious duty even when faced with very serious crime against the state, still a perfectly good hot potato. Of course, all art exists in dialogue with its audience and the changing nature of that dialogue in different times and places, but to do true justice to a work one must always first know the context in which it was created and meant to be understood. While the world of the ancient Greeks may seem so familiar to us, there are many ways in which their assumptions, prejudices and comprehensions differ widely from the assumptions, prejudices and comprehensions of our own little slot in time. How were crowds on their stone seats on the hillside with the sun in their eyes reacting when Hippolytos thought he could get away with ignoring Aphrodite?

It is possible to recognise simply from a ground plan whether a theatre is the untouched original Classical Greek version, a Hellenistic structure or adaptation or a Roman structure or adaptation. The Greeks always built their theatres into hillsides and the circular orchestra was an essential component of the original productions. Some adaptation is made in the Hellenistic, when the orchestra becomes D-shaped, and then the Romans, who had mastered the arch and load-bearing in a way that the Greeks - for all their extraordinary understanding of proportion and perspective - did not, built free standing theatres with semi-circular orchestras which are now not performance space but the stalls. (If you put two free-standing theatres together you get an amphitheatre, but you will not find these in the Greek areas of the Roman empire because even under those masters the Greeks never developed a taste for inventive public execution as a good day's entertainment.) If a theatre is built into a hill but has a semi-circular orchestra and substantial stage buildings you may be sure that the Romans took it over and adapted it.

This is, in fact, the fate of the Theatre of Dionysos in Athens, which is where the great works would first have been seen.

The Athenians decided on building a permanent theatre after the collapse of wooden seating set up in the Agora (major public space) in Athens. The theatre sits tucked under the Acropolis (there is a later Roman theatre farther down the road, do not confuse the two), with seating arranged like orange segments, with a couple of circular paths easing access to different levels. Seating was wood at first then stone. Certain important people, including the priest of Dionysos, had special seats right at the front and in many theatres you can still see the inscriptions identifying whose places these should be. The seating surrounds perhaps two-thirds of the orchestra leaving room for access passages, *parodoi* (singular, *parodos,* you may also see these referred to as *eisodoi*), to either side. The chorus would use these to enter and leave, and so at times could the actors – traditionally you would leave for town in one direction (stage left) and country in the other (stage right).

In front and closing off the end of the theatre were the stage and stage buildings - originally wooden and low, they became more substantial and grandiose over the centuries, but were originally quite simple. This is where the actors will spend much of their time and all this means that they are a long way from the audience - if you were sitting at the back in the Theatre of Dionysos you would be no less than 300 feet from the action. Subtlety of acting was simply not an available option, although the magnificence of Greek theatre acoustics meant that the poetry was not lost to the air. Those who have enjoyed the spectacle but not the sound quality of open-air productions should really try to experience a performance in a Greek theatre, it will be a revelation.

By the standards of the typical modern theatre, the major Greek theatres are enormous. A large opera house today might have a capacity of a couple of thousand. The Theatre of Dionysos seated around 14,000 - and it is not the biggest theatre in the Greek world by any means. These were not intimate spaces, and modern televisual acting styles would be simply unimaginable. It is not just stage acting, but stadium acting.

The stage itself, the *proskenion* (pronounced prawskaynion), which comes out in a Latinised version as the familiar word proscenium, was originally a temporary structure. The original stage at the Theatre of Dionysos was about 60 feet long – the dimensions changed over time. The depth was narrow, probably about ten feet. It was low, possibly not even as much as two feet high, and this was important because from time to time the actors do have to get up and down from the orchestra. Beautifully painted pottery was a major export from Athens and it is a hugely valuable archaeological resource in many areas, not least theatre. We do, for example, have illustration of a low wooden stage with steps up from ground level.

Behind the *proskenion* was the stage building, the *skene* (pronounced skaynay). This was quite a modest wooden building in its original version, longer than the stage platform itself, but still quite narrow, not much deeper than the stage itself, despite having to house props and changing areas. Traditionally, there would be three doors from the stage into the building, which could serve as a palace, a temple or even Philoktetes' cave. Only a few props could be used, or one single painted backdrop per production, as there was no opportunity for scene change and this would anyway defy the unity of place. (A very few plays do change from one setting to another, but this is rare and there would need to be a very quick way to convey this - a good argument for keeping the background very simple.) Things do get more elaborate as the 5th. century wore on, and scene-painting for the theatre came to affect interior decoration in Athens, but there is always the inescapable practicality of what can and cannot be done given the physical circumstances of production.

A small temple was tucked behind the *skene* and temples will be found in close proximity to other theatres across the Greek world. The beautiful little temple to the side of the spectacular (and dizzying) theatre high on the hillside in Pergamon is one of my personal favourites.

The roof of the *skene* could become an acting area in limited circumstances, e.g. a watchman on the roof introducing the action in a prologue. This higher level would generally be the domain of higher beings, and the stage business of gods as characters in plays has passed into our language. There would be a crane on the roof, the *mechane* (pronounced me*ch*anay, Scottish ch again), the Latin for which is *machina*. The *deus ex machina* is literally the god on the crane, although he/she would regularly simply appear on the roof area (the *theologeion*, pronounced theolog eye on). Typically the god would appear at the end to mete out justice and/or explain what has happened and will happen, hence the development of the modern meaning. Euripides rather often uses this device as a bit of a short-cut to wrap things up when he has explored all the scenes that interest him in the play and wants to draw it all to a close, but it can be a powerful moment in the denouement. Humans were not supposed to be able to see gods in their true form (much unpleasantness could ensue), so this mechanism was a neat way of emphasising the difference between human and divine and solving a staging issue at one and the same time. The *mechane* could well have been used in *Hippolytos* (otherwise the goddesses would appear on the *theologeion*). Humans could be carried by the *mechane* sometimes, one spectacular example being the escape of Medeia.

There can also, of course, be interventions from below such as the ghost of Dareios appearing to his son, Xerxes, in *Persai*. Ghosts or underworld deities would not appear above, so it is believed there could be some trapdoor mechanism to allow them to manifest as needed.

One important piece of stage machinery, and one that is particularly assisted in creating *coups de theatre* by the siting of the Theatre of Dionysos in Athens which means that the sun is in the audience's eyes, is the *ekkuklema* (pronounced engkouklayma). This was a low platform that could be rolled out from the *skene* with a tableau e.g. of the corpses of Medeia's children, or the corpse of Agamemnon. Because in the theatre in which these plays were originally staged it was not possible to see into the darkness behind the central doors, this allowed for real dramatic impact. Theatres around the Greek world thereafter would face in different directions, but no doubt care was taken to ensure these moments continue to hold their power. This device fits perfectly with the way the Greeks dealt with the actual horror. Quite apart from the special effects issue, it would have been unacceptable to them actually to view the violence, which would provoke the wrong kinds of emotion whether that be disgust or titillation. It is powerful and effective enough to hear about it (producers of torture porn might take note here), and messenger speeches describing the awful events, be it battle, madness or murder, are some of the best set-pieces of Greek drama. The odd less-disturbing violent act, such as the suicide of Aias (Ajax) could be seen on stage, but managed discreetly.

Other effects could be possible with fairly simple ingredients, e.g. rolling stones in a barrel provides pretty effective thunder. We know flame effects were sometimes used, although we do not know how – smoke itself would be no problem.

Actors in tragedy would wear buskins, boots which could fit either foot, masks and elaborate costumes, so that even the most harrowing of tales would be good to look at. When Euripides brought people on in rags it caused almost as much outrage as some of his disturbing themes and characters. These elements did serve also very practical purposes. As we have seen, Greek theatres were enormous and therefore being able to identify and understand figures at the nearest about 60 feet away was essential. There were archetypal masks (which would include the hair) for a range of different characters, from hero to old crone, and there would be props that would instantly signal that the audience was looking at e.g. Zeus with a thunderbolt, a herald with a wreath or a traveller with a wide-brimmed *petasos* hat.

Attending a day of drama at festival time must have been a profound experience, which was part of the benefit for Aristotle, as working through all that emotion achieves *catharsis,* cleansing - the very word we use today - although for Aristotle the benefits were not just clearing out the individual psyche but actually a cleansing of the body politic and therefore a reduction in the danger of the one thing the Athenians dreaded above all - *stasis*, civil unrest. The performances would start in the early morning and by the time one had sat through the three tragedies per day with all their splendour of music, dance and drama and then the emotional release of a jolly romp of a satyr play (very little indeed remains of these), probably fortified by picnics and wineskins, and all in the company of a large crowd, one would have gone through something powerful. Modern audiences are entranced, entertained, shocked, gripped by just one play at a time. Perhaps one could try to imagine a mixture of Glastonbury (the festival), Glyndebourne and Glastonbury (the Christian pilgrimage), with stone seats.

Getting the plays to the theatre was a carefully managed process. Funding the production was a public service, a liturgy, which was the way the Athenians avoided exacting taxation from the citizen population at large (they were happy to tax non-citizens). To perform a liturgy was both a burden and an honour, others included e.g. the funding of a trireme, a warship. Someone of sufficient financial standing would be appointed by the Eponymous Archon (one of the top offices of the Athenian state) as *choregos* and assigned to one of the three chosen dramatists, each of whom would need to produce four plays for his day of the festival: three dramas (usually unrelated) and a satyr play. The *choregos* would need to cover the costs of rehearsal, costuming, musicians, and all production and when it came to prize time it is he who would get the most significant award. Monuments to successful *choregoi* are still to be seen at the Theatre of Dionysos and in the streets of Athens. It is believed there would be some choice over the actors in the 5th. Century, with the best hotly pursued, but by the 4th. Century at least the protagonist may have been assigned as well. Some of the playwrights were capable actors, but they certainly needed to be multi-talented as they were not only responsible for the deathless poetry through which we now know them but also direction, choreography and music. And all this for one day in one of the only two festivals in the year when drama was produced (plays did thereafter get taken round to rural festivals, read and disseminated across the Greek world, but they were never put on again in the Athens of the time). At the end of the Great Dionysia there would be a day with five comedies. The Lenaia was a shorter festival later in the year. Originally entrance was free, but when a small charge was introduced so was a state fund to enable as many as possible to take part in the festival.

The dramatists, remember, were always in competition. The process for judging this was complex in a typically Athenian way. They had a paranoia about eliminating any possibility of cheating (and if the following seems a touch extreme, do take time to discover the mindbending lengths, including something akin to the invention of pinball, to which they went to try to eliminate any possibility of jury-nobbling in the courts). A list of potential judges was drawn up from the ten tribes of citizens (just accept this - getting one's head around the socio-political organisation of Athens requires time and diagrams) and these names were placed into ten urns which were then sealed and held until the festival, when the urns were brought out, checked for signs of tampering and then a name drawn from each urn, producing the ten judges. After they had seen all three days of tragedy each judge would write down his choice of first, second and third and place this in an urn. Then a random five of the individual verdicts would be withdrawn, and these would be used for the eventual decision. We have no idea what criteria other than personal taste, prejudice or whim the judges may have been expected to use. Some of the decisions of which we are aware seem bizarre, e.g. *Oidipous the Tyrant*, that paradigm of dramatic excellence, did not win, for all Sophokles was enormously popular as a person and contributor to Athenian life - but we do not know so many of the different circumstances of the production. Perhaps on that occasion Sophokles did not do himself justice with the other plays for that particular day (the Theban plays were not written as a trilogy, and were in fact written many years apart), perhaps the actors or the chorus let him down (although I have never seen this play fail, whether performed by schoolboys or a stellar cast), perhaps the *choregos* had been stingy with the costumes, perhaps the rival who won had provided a really strong programme we would still be enjoying now had any of those plays survived - there are so many variables we have absolutely no way of checking.

The judgement of millions of playgoers and scholars ever since has been quite clear. The three great men of Athenian drama produced, in the course of about 70 years when they were at work, some of the greatest drama the world ever has or ever will see. It lives in the consciousness even of people who have not heard their names and will live on to enrich and expand the minds of generations to come.

STAGING NOTES AND REMINDERS

Stage directions do not feature in the texts of Greek dramas - the poets themselves were there to act as directors or actors. One has to work from the raw text, and that is what is given here. Imagine an opera libretto with no stage directions and no score. There would by Euripides' time be three actors maximum in speaking roles, although occasionally there is a fourth silent actor in a scene, and they had to share roles. The modern director must work out whether to have one actor per character or, if keeping to the smaller cast, work out precisely when the changes are made. This has the plus point of forcing close attention to the text, and also the dramatic impact that some scenes will change depending on how the movement of characters is interpreted. Some problems are automatically resolved - as they were at the time - if the actors are in masks, which is always a powerful experience and well worth considering not only because it is authentic but because of the gifts and demands that masks provide for both audience and performer. It is not just about physical acting styles: the audience will read expressions in blank masks - try it to see how true that apparent nonsense is.

While it is not now generally believed that the masks would act as a kind of megaphone, they did have an extremely practical purpose in the settings of huge outdoor Greek theatres which were designed for audiences not of hundreds, but of thousands. Everything you may have heard about the extraordinary acoustics of these glorious hillsides is perfectly true, but the back of a Greek theatre is a long, long way from the action. Masks are quickly identifiable, even more so as there were certain standard types, such as wise old man, young *maiden, strapping hero and so on, so that people with no programme notes could get immediately into the story - aided by the sort of necessary scene-setting explanations in the text saying who is speaking and where. Scene painting developed over the course of the 5th. Century B.C. and came to influence home interior decoration (even more so in the Roman period), but there is still a limit to what could be done - the pictures have to come from the words. This does not mean the audience always knew what was going to happen - they may know about the characters, but not what this poet was about to do with them.*

One interesting and worthwhile mixture of ancient and modern conventions can be to leave the main characters unmasked but mask the chorus. This can act as a visual reminder of the vital but different roles of actor and chorus and is one of the satisfying compromises.

In terms of staging, the Greek theatre consisted of a low stage with three doors opening into the building (here palace) at the back and circular orchestra (dancing floor) in front. As a rule of thumb, you can date a theatre by the shape of the orchestra: circular = Classical, D-shaped = Hellenistic, semi-circle = Roman and at that point part of the seating, not the action. The place of the actors is largely, though not entirely, on the stage. The chorus never leaves the orchestra, although in this play Euripides teases us with the possibility that they might. How this is interpreted in a modern production will in part depend on the stage available.

That the chorus has a large space to play with is actually vital for reminding modern interpreters and audiences of its vital role - Greek theatre was total theatre, all-singing, all-dancing. The chorus nowadays is all too often reduced to one person dressed in black and while, yes, the action being observed and commented on can be potently dark stuff, the chorus in the original would be sumptuously dressed (until

Euripides) and singing. They would not always be en bloc - they would divide to dance and sing antiphonally and the leader would sometimes go solo in engaging with the actors. Budget and time obviously affect choices here, but there is a lot of scope for using the chorus in new and exciting ways and splitting text amongst them for best effect. One interesting production I have seen allowed the chorus the freedom to decide on a random basis who would say (always remember it would originally be sing, not say) any part, with break points at any point of punctuation. It was remarkably effective in creating a sense of oneness in the chorus, but does require an input of rehearsal and confidence that may be too daunting for most productions - there is always the risk of the spreading disease, well known to anyone experienced in choral singing or speaking, of being unable to get the first note out, and then everything falls apart. No-one should ever feel that he or she is 'only' in the chorus in any Greek play because that would be completely to misunderstand Greek drama. The challenging elements in this particular play should provoke particularly interesting discussion. A crucial area in which it is unique is that there is a suggestion in the ambiguous fragmentary passage that is regularly omitted from translations that there could be an extra chorus in the middle of the work. No-one really understands this, but I have included the text in its entirety nonetheless. Deal with it as you see best. It is already unprecedented that one chorus appears at the start and then must have to disappear sharpish before the chorus that will be there throughout the rest of the action gets to dance in. The other unique element is the teasing suggestion that the chorus might be about to make a difference. They stick to convention and do not, but it does offer an interesting element to play with in production.

The only scenery suggestion I would give is that there ought to be statues or altars of Aphrodite and Artemis near the house, *as the images are addressed. The gods are not visible to humans - even Hippolytos, favourite of Artemis, can only hear and not see her. These statues would most likely be in the orchestra in the original production where there would already be an altar to Dionysos. Should your production area run to an accessible roof or a crane then the gods could appear to the audience in the traditional Greek way, literally on an upper plane.*

For the purposes of people using this translation for Classical Studies, I have used transliteration of the Greek for the main text, as has been becoming ever more popular – and rightly so. Drama students might be a little more disconcerted by the unfamiliar and more alien-looking spellings (and a quick lesson on the Greek alphabet might help a lot here), so I have included in the Guide to Names and Places the Latin versions which may feel a lot more comfortable and may be easier to contemplate saying. If this is being undertaken as a joint Classics/Drama project then do try to go with the original versions. There are some rather ugly interpretations of the sounds of Greek about these days - the older standard sound values both conform rather better to the Latinised versions that have come down to us traditionally, and are easier to say (the educated Roman will have been pretty much bilingual and anyone with business in the Eastern Mediterranean will have been at least competent in Greek, which was the lingua franca *of the area). You will need, however, to be guided by the language specialists you have to hand.*

I have translated entirely in prose - it is extremely difficult to translate poetry, even more so to render it in poetry, and that should be left to actual poets. Students of Greek will find a literal translation of more immediate use than a freer poetic one.

I have not made any distinction between passages that would be sung (choral interludes, arias and duets) and spoken passages. I keep emphasising that Greek drama is really grand opera, with reflective arias (any long speech would actually be sung), passages of the quick-fire stichomythia *dialogue advancing the action and performing a similar function to recitative, and choral passages both sung and danced commenting on it all and acting as audience and everyman. This should help the modern student and scholar to understand just how shocking it was when Euripides presented his form of what would have felt like 'kitchen sink' drama with realistic costuming, depressing staging and all-too-real subtexts, rather than epic grandeur and splendour providing some cushion against the agonies being explored. But then again, his choruses were smash hits. It is up to director and cast to decide whether to add music or rhythm. The texts are strong enough to withstand changes in types of staging, and budget constraints will no doubt feature in any decisions.*

I have added directions such as (cries out), *to try to render the powerful but untranslatable cries of anguish in the original Greek. Occasionally I have translated these by the modern instinctive English cry of 'No!' or Oh, no!'. Director and cast can work out in each case what appears natural for the production.*

Final reminders - this is a play about divine forces. It is also a play about warped personalities and unhappy families, but remember that for the Greek world you cannot just reduce it to Freud and secular hang-ups. The religious dimension is supremely important. Hippolytos is offending the divine force without which life cannot be. He is also defying his duties as a man - because in the Greek world the individual only has a place as part of society - and as a scion of the royal house. He does not fit in to the human world, and has committed sacrilege against the divine world. The version in which Phaidra was a willing seducer was a flop. The version you are looking at now won its contest and has been studied and staged ever since.

THε MΛƧKƧ IN THε ꝹRΛMΛ

Dramatos Prosopa
(i.e. Dramatis Personae)

Really, literally- that is what it means. The mask tells the audience what kind of character to expect to start with, then whom it represents in this particular play.

Aphrodite - Goddess of love, but this is something more raw, goddess of sex, creation and generation is more like it.

Hippolytos - Bastard son of Theseus and the Amazon, Hippolyta. He rejects sexuality and refuses to acknowledge Aphrodite. Offending the gods, arrogance, going beyond that which the gods allow (*hubris*) always leads to *nemesis* in Greek drama (the justified indignation of the gods) and leads to *ate* (ruin and also the madness that ensures you come to ruin). Once the gods are out to get you, they will make sure that you commit the final act that condemns you.

A chorus of huntsmen - They appear with Hippolytos at the beginning of the play and then go off, *possibly* to re-appear when Hippolytos is banished by his father. It is otherwise unheard of to have more than one chorus.

Servants - In the Ancient World servants will be slaves (or a slave who has been freed if old/loyal/good at saving-up for it enough and in good favour). That is everyday normality. In the Greek world they are integral members of the *oikos*, the house/household which is the basic unit of Greek society and an enormously powerful concept in Greek thought and culture, and are as much caught up in its fate as its more prominent members. Any loyalty, affection, concern expressed between

42

household slave and master or mistress in drama should be seen as quite genuine feeling.

A chorus of women of Troizen (pronounced Troydzayn) - The main chorus of this play. Conventionally they observe but cannot affect the plot, although Euripides' pushes the boundaries of this convention here.

The Nurse - To what extent she is just a plain old peasant woman who cannot be bothered with all this aristocratic worrying about honour, or is primarily just worried about her beloved charge, or is a wicked old pander, is up to the director and cast to decide.

Phaidra - She is desperately trying to do the right thing in face of the power of the goddess. Aphrodite has nothing against her, she just needs a tool for her attack on Hippolytos. The concepts of honour, keeping within the appropriate bounds, preserving face - these are vital to a Heroic culture (think Samurai, Knights of the Round Table, Klingons). When all else fails there is only honour and a good name left.

Theseus - Well-known hero and King of Athens. There are old family connections to Troizen, which is why he has come here during his voluntary exile, and why Hippolytos has been brought up here, following a Heroic practice similar to the Mediaeval English practice of sending the sons of nobility to learn the nobleman's trade in other houses. He alludes to a range of his adventures in beating up nasty bandits on the Isthmus, and his voyage to Crete to slay Phaidra's half-brother, the Minotaur, which led to his breaking the heart of Phaidra's sister, Ariadne, who helped him and whom he then dumped on the island of Naxos (it turned out all right, Dionysos found her and liked what he saw). He is seen in this play as both the son of Poseidon and the son of Aigeus, King of Athens. Never mind the logic - just accept the story.

A Messenger - Messenger speeches are regularly the great set pieces of Greek drama and Messenger is therefore a plum role. One is not disturbed, disgusted or titillated by actually seeing the violent action, but one hears all about it. Consider how effectively this works upon the imagination (it also solves the special effects problem).

Artemis - Virgin goddess of the hunt, who also looks after women in childbirth (a seriously dangerous experience for Greek women). Only a goddess can resolve such a dichotomy and Hippolytos can only solve his problem of being a grown-up who rejects sexuality by dying and having a hero-cult set up in his name.

HIPPOLYTOS

APHRODITE   Great among mortals and not without a name in Heaven, I am called Aphrodite, the Cyprian. As many as live from the Black Sea to the boundaries of the Atlantic and see the light of the sun, I give precedence to those who revere my power. I throw down those who think themselves too high for me. For it is in the nature of gods to rejoice in being honoured by mankind.

I shall show you quickly the story of these things: Hippolytos, the son of Theseus, borne by the Amazon, educated by the upright Pittheus, alone amongst the citizens of the land of Troizen calls me the worst of divine powers. He shrinks from sex and has no truck with marriage. He honours Artemis, sister of Phoibos Apollo and daughter of Zeus, believing her the greatest of divinities. Always together with her in the green wood, and with his swift hounds, he clears the earth of beasts - having fallen into greater than mortal company. Now, I do not envy him these things - for what need have I? For the things he has done to wrong me, I shall punish Hippolytos this very day. Many things have long been set in motion - I do not need to do much work.

For when he once went from the revered house of Pittheus to see and complete his initiation into the Mysteries of Pandion's land of Athens, his father's noble wife, Phaidra, saw him and a terrible love, by my plans, seized her heart.

Before she came to this land of Troizen, she built on that rock of Pallas, looking towards this land, a temple to Cyprian Aphrodite, thinking of her absent beloved. It will be established with the name of Hippolytos in the future. When Theseus left the land of Kekrops, fleeing blood-guilt because of the Pallantides, and sailed with his wife to this land, having agreed to a year in exile, here the wretched woman, groaning and desperate with the goads of love, is dying and in silence. No-one in the household knows her illness. But this love must not culminate like that. I shall show Theseus how things stand, and all will become clear. His father will kill that young man, my enemy, with curses that Poseidon, Lord of the Sea, gave to Theseus - he would not ask the god three times in vain. Phaidra shall keep her good name, but will die all the same. For I shall not let her suffering outweigh what is prepared for my enemies, so that I shall have all the justice that seems good to me.

But - I see Hippolytos, son of Theseus, marching along, having left the toils of hunting. I shall leave this place. Many followers are with him, making a great noise with hymns to honour Artemis. He does not know that the gates of Hades are open and this is the last light he will see.

HIPPOLYTOS   Follow, singing, follow heavenly Artemis, daughter of Zeus, to whom we are devoted.

CHORUS OF HUNTSMEN   Lady, most holy lady, daughter of Zeus, hail, hail, Oh, Artemis, daughter of Leto and Zeus, - most beautiful of maidens, who dwells in the noble hall of high heaven, the golden home of Zeus. Hail, Artemis, most beautiful maiden of Olympos.

HIPPOLYTOS   For you, mistress, I bring this twined garland from an unmown meadow as adornment. There no shepherd thinks fit to graze his flock, nor came any sickle, but the bee in spring passes through the untouched meadow. Purity makes a garden with pure streams of river water; those who are untaught but whom by nature wisdom has wholly enwrapped may harvest - for the wicked it is not sanctioned. Beloved mistress, receive from a reverent hand a band for your golden hair. For this gift is for me alone among mortals to keep company with you and exchange words, hearing your voice though I do not see your face. May I make the last turn in my life as I began.

SERVANT   Lord - for only gods should be called masters - will you take a piece of good advice from me?

HIPPOLYTOS   Certainly, or I would not appear wise.

SERVANT   You know, then, the law laid down for mortals ...

HIPPOLYTOS   I don't know. What is it you are asking me about?

SERVANT   ... to hate pride and being exclusive.

HIPPOLYTOS   Indeed that is right; which proud man is not a vexation to people?

SERVANT   In being affable there is a certain grace?

HIPPOLYTOS   Very much, and gain too, with little effort.

SERVANT   And do you look for the same amongst the gods?

HIPPOLYTOS   If mortals use the same laws as the gods.

SERVANT   Then why do you not address a proud deity?

HIPPOLYTOS   Which one? Be careful your mouth does not get you into trouble.

SERVANT   This one *[indicates statue]*, the Cyprian who stands at your gate.

HIPPOLYTOS   I who am pure greet her from afar.

SERVANT   Yet she is proud and distinguished among mortals.

HIPPOLYTOS   One may care for different things, amongst gods or men.

SERVANT   You need to be lucky, and keep a sound mind.

HIPPOLYTOS   None of the gods admired at night pleases me.

SERVANT   Son, the gods must have their honour.

HIPPOLYTOS   Go on, men, go into the house and eat. A laden table is pleasing after the hunt, and the horses must be rubbed down so that you can yoke them into the chariot, and after a good dinner I'll have some good exercise. You can keep your Cyprian goddess.

SERVANT   It's not for us to imitate young men when they think this way - as it befits slaves to speak, we pray before your statues, Mistress Aphrodite. You must excuse if someone says foolish things out of the arrogance of youth. You should not listen to these things - gods ought to be wiser than men.

CHORUS *[Troizenian women unless specified otherwise]*   It is said there is an overhanging rock dripping with water, an abundant source for filling pitchers. There a friend of mine was soaking purple cloaks in the running stream then laid them down on the hot, sunny surface of the rocks. There the first word came to me about the mistress.

She keeps inside the house, in distress, on a sick bed, covering her golden head with a fine veil. I hear that for three days now her mouth has taken no food, she has kept her body pure from Demeter's corn. She keeps the reason for her grief hidden, and longs for the unhappy ending of death.

Are you seized by a god, lady, Pan or Hekate, the mad wanderings the Mother of the Mountains sends on the ecstatic Korybantes? Did you sin against Diktynna, the mighty huntress, by neglecting her, are you wasting away for not offering her sacrifice? For she wanders on the shores, or dry land, as well as on the salt whirlpools of the sea.

Or is your noble husband, foremost of the sons of Erechtheus, grazing in the pastures of a secret bed? Or has some man set sail from Crete for this harbour, friendly to sailors, bringing a message to the queen, causing grief so that her bed has become her life?

A miserable impossibility lives in the perverse temperament of women, causing agonies of unreasonable thoughts. A wind once shot through my womb, but I called on the heavenly helper of women, Artemis of the arrows, the one who aids women in childbirth, and she always comes - may she be praised among the gods.

But here is the old Nurse, before the doors, bringing Phaidra out of the house. The gloomy cloud of her brow is increasing. My soul longs to know what has harmed and changed the body of the queen.

NURSE   Oh, what hateful ills afflict mankind! What shall I do? What shall I not do? Here you are in the bright light, under the open sky - we have brought your sick-bed out of the house. Your every word was for coming here, soon you will be hurrying back to your room again. Things quickly cheat you, and nothing gives you pleasure. What you have does not satisfy you, you would rather have something else. It's better to be ill than do the nursing: the one is a single trouble, the other vexes the heart and the hands. The whole of man's life is painful, and there is no end to troubles. But if there is another, better life, it hides from us in clouds of surrounding darkness. We love, if not wisely, what appears to us as a glitter of being on the earth, because we know of no other life, and there is not proof of what it is like below the earth. We are carried away aimlessly with stories.

PHAIDRA   Raise my body, set straight my head. I have lost the strength of my limbs. Servants, take hold of my lovely arms. My head-dress is heavy on my head - take it off, let my hair cover my shoulders.

NURSE   Have courage, child, don't make things difficult by tossing and turning. You will bear the illness easily with a peaceful heart and a will appropriate to your noble birth. Mortals have to suffer.

PHAIDRA   (groans) How may I take a draught of pure water from a dewy fountain, lie and rest under the black poplars in the grassy meadow?

NURSE   Child, what are you saying? Don't say such things, throwing out words borne on madness in front of the people.

PHAIDRA   Send me to the mountain; I shall go to the forest and through the pines, where the dogs run, ready for the kill, pressing hard on the spotted deer. By the gods, I am on heat to shout to the dogs, to throw a Thessalian lance next to my flowing golden hair, holding a barbed weapon in my hand.

NURSE   Why ever are you fretting for these things, child? What has hunting with hounds to do with you? Why do you crave flowing spring water? There is a dewy cliff near the walls where you can get a drink.

PHAIDRA   Mistress Artemis of the salt sea-shore, and of the trained horsemen, if only I could be on your plains, controlling Thessalian colts.

NURSE   What is this madness you are coming out with? A minute ago you wanted to go off to the mountains to the hunt, and now you want a dry track for horses. This really needs a seer, child, to find out which of the gods is driving you off the track and takes away your senses.

PHAIDRA   Wretch that I am, whatever have I done? How far have I wandered from my right mind? I was mad - a god's ruin fell upon me. Oh, I am in misery! Nurse, hide my head again, for I am ashamed of the things I have been saying. Cover me. Tears come to my eyes. My face is turned in shame. It is painful to regain one's right mind, but evil to be mad. It is better to die not knowing anything.

NURSE   I'm covering you. When will death hide my body? I have lived a long time and learnt many things. It is better to be moderate in mixing the bowl of friendship with other mortals, and not go to the very marrow of the soul, thoughts of love are easily dissolved, to let go or hold together. For one soul to bear the pain of two, as I suffer for her, is a heavy burden. They say that cultivating precise and scrupulous refinements in life causes you to fall rather than brings pleasure, and is actually an enemy to health. So I think 'Moderation in all things' is better than being too much the slave, and the wise will agree with me.

CHORUS   Old woman, faithful nurse to the queen, we see Phaidra's miserable fortune, but it is not clear to us what the illness is. We should like to hear about it from you.

NURSE   I don't know the story; she doesn't want to talk.

CHORUS   Not how these troubles started?

NURSE   You have come to the same thing, for she keeps completely silent.

CHORUS   How weak and wasted her body is!

NURSE   How would it not be - she has not eaten for three days.

CHORUS   Is this madness sent by a god to ruin her, or is she trying to die?

NURSE   To die? She is going without food to depart from life.

CHORUS   You are telling quite a story if her husband is ready to accept this.

NURSE   She hides her suffering and does not say she is ill.

CHORUS   Does he not recognise it by looking at her face?

NURSE   He happens to be away from home, out of the country.

CHORUS   You should hold out your hands, try to find out what causes this illness and wandering wits.

NURSE   I have tried everything and can get nothing to work, but I shall not give up, and am willing to try again, because you are here and can bear witness with me how I have behaved towards my unlucky mistress.

Come, dear child, let us both forget the words we said before, and you be sweeter, relax your gloomy brow, and the path of your thoughts, and I, where I did not understand you well, will turn to another, better argument. If your illness is one of those that should not be mentioned, these women can help with treatment. If it can be divulged and brought before men, speak, so that the problem can be shown to doctors.

Well? Why are you silent? You should not be silent, child, but if I am not saying the right things, chastise me, or agree if I am speaking well.

Say something! Look at me! Oh, how miserable I am. Women, we labour at these toils in vain, we are going back to where we were before, for she was not softened by words then and now too she will not be persuaded.

Yet, know this - if you become more stubborn than the sea, if you die, you are betraying your sons; they will not have a share of their father's house. No, by the riding lady Amazon, Hippolyta, who bore a proud bastard who will be master to your children, you know him well - Hippolytos.

PHAIDRA   Oh, no!

NURSE   Does that touch you?

PHAIDRA   You will kill me, Nurse. I beg you, by the gods, do not speak about that man again.

NURSE   Do you see? You are in your right mind, but still you do not want to help your sons or save your life.

PHAIDRA   I love my children, but I am distressed by a different fortune.

NURSE   Daughter, are you hands pure from blood?

PHAIDRA   My hands are pure, it is my heart that carries a pollution.

NURSE   Surely not from some baneful enemy?

PHAIDRA   Someone close kills me, by neither my will nor his.

NURSE   Has Theseus harmed you with some wrong?

PHAIDRA   May I do him no evil turn.

NURSE   Then what is this terrible thing that makes you want to die?

PHAIDRA   I sin! But I do not sin against you.

NURSE   Of course not willingly, but it will be your fault if I am left behind.

[In taking Phaidra's hand and then grasping her knees the Nurse is following the normal Greek practices of making supplication, she will later try some of the same with Hippolytos.]

PHAIDRA   What are you doing? Do you force me, hanging on to my hand?

NURSE   And your knees, and I will never let you go.

PHAIDRA   It would be bad for you, poor woman, if you found out.

NURSE   What could be bad for me worse than what is happening to you?

PHAIDRA   It would destroy you. The matter bears on my honour.

NURSE   Why then are you hiding when I am right to come to you as a suppliant?

PHAIDRA   I am trying to engineer something noble out of shameful things.

NURSE   Then you will appear more worthy of honour by speaking.

PHAIDRA   By the gods, go away and let go of my right hand.

NURSE   No, I won't. You are not giving me the gift you ought.

PHAIDRA   I shall give it. For I have reverence for your ritual hand.

NURSE   I shall be silent now, it is your story from here.

PHAIDRA   Oh, what a pitiful love you had, mother!

NURSE   The one she had for the bull, child? Why are you talking about this?

PHAIDRA   And you too, my poor sister, consort of Dionysos.

NURSE   Child, what is the matter with you? You say dreadful things about your family.

PHAIDRA   I am the third accursed one as I die.

NURSE   This is a blow to me. Where is your story leading?

PHAIDRA   My misfortunes come from there, they are not new.

NURSE   You are still telling me nothing of what I want to hear.

PHAIDRA   Is there any way you could say for me what I have to say?

NURSE   I am not a seer to know clearly what is hidden.

PHAIDRA   What is it, when people say they love?

NURSE   The sweetest thing, daughter, but painful at the same time.

PHAIDRA   I stand in need of one of them.

NURSE   What are you saying? Are you in love with some man, child?

PHAIDRA   He is that man, the Amazon's ...

NURSE   You mean Hippolytos?

PHAIDRA   You said it, you did not hear it from me!

NURSE   Oh, no, what are you going to say, child? You will destroy me. Women, do not bear it - I cannot live with it. Hateful day, I see a hateful light! I cast myself down, don't touch me. Dying, I release myself from life. Farewell! I am no more. Those with wisdom and discretion are falling into lust despite themselves. Aphrodite is not a goddess, but is something greater than a god. She has destroyed this woman, and me, and the house.

CHORUS   Did you hear, did you not hear the cries of the terrible suffering of the queen? Let me die, before you come to your purpose. This is dreadful. Wretched one, daughter of these pains - Oh, trouble, nurse of mortals! You are destroyed, you have displayed evil things to the light. What waits for you throughout all the day? Some new end awaits the house. Aphrodite's fortune, which wastes you away, is no longer unknown, unhappy daughter of Crete.

PHAIDRA   Women of Troizen, who live at the farthest portal of the land of Pelops, I have at times thought for long in the night of lives of men which have been destroyed. It seems to me that this does not happen because of a naturally wicked mind, for many of them have good hearts. But one must consider this: we know and recognise what is best, but do not carry it out, some from idleness, others placing pleasure above doing right. There are many pleasures in life, long talks, leisure, guilty pleasure, modesty. There are two of these, one does no harm, the other is a burden to the house. If it were clear which was the right one, they would not both be written the same way. As this is what I happen to think myself, I do not know what kind of drug could change this or make me take the opposite opinion. I shall tell you the path of my thoughts. When love struck me, I looked to find how best I could endure it. So I began in this way, keeping silent and hiding my affliction. One cannot place trust in the tongue, that opening knows how to advise the hearts of men and lays the worst evils on itself. Secondly, I resolved to be triumphant by bearing this madness with self-discipline. Thirdly, when by these means I could not rule unruly Aphrodite, it seemed to me the best of my plans, beyond contradiction, to die. I would not wish my good deeds to be forgotten or my shameful ones to have many witnesses. I knew the deed and the ailment were both dis-honourable, I knew well that I am a woman, an object of hate to all. May every evil destroy her, whoever first shamed her bed with interlopers. This evil began with women from the noble houses. For when doing shameful things seems fine to the noble-born, it is going to seem to fine to the ordinary people. I hate those who are prudent in speech but dare evil deeds in secret. However, Aphrodite, mistress of the sea, do they look into the faces of their husbands or shiver in case the conspiratorial darkness or chamber might find a voice?

I am dying for this, friends, so that I shall never bring shame to my husband or the children I bore. But may they live free and speak freely in Athens, city of renown, with a mother of good reputation. For it can make even the bold-hearted man a slave if he knows evil things about mother or father. They say one thing only is available for the struggle with life, a just and decent mind. Time shows the evils of men, happen when it will, like a young girl in front of a mirror. May I never be seen amongst them!

CHORUS   Self-discipline is noble everywhere and bears the fruit of a noble glory amongst men.

NURSE   Mistress, when I heard of your circumstances just now I suddenly had a terrible fear, but now I have it in mind that I was not thinking it through. For mortals, second thoughts tend to be wiser. Nothing in your story is out of the ordinary. The passions of the goddess have fallen upon you. You are in love. Where is the wonder in that? You have it in common with many mortals. Are you destroying your life for love? Is it not a poor look-out for your fellow creatures who love, and those to come, if they have to die? Aphrodite is not to be withstood when she pours down upon you. She comes peacefully upon those who yield, when she finds a know-it-all she treats him badly. Aphrodite wanders in the ether, she is in the swell of the sea, all things spring from her. She is the one who sows seeds and gives desire from which issue all of us on earth. Whoever have writings from olden times and are always amongst the Muses know that Zeus once loved Semele, they also know that beautifully-shining Dawn once snatched up Kephalos to the heavens because of love. But now they live in heaven and do not flee out of the way of the gods. They are vanquished by circumstances but are, I think, contented.

But you do not give in? Your father should have made conditions when he made you, or under the rule of different gods, if you will not accept these laws. How many sensible husbands, do you think, see things wrong in their beds but appear not to see? How many fathers help their sinning sons to carry out their love affairs? This is wise for men, to let things that are not good escape notice. It is not appropriate for mortals to struggle for too much in life. You don't have to finish off the roof or the covering of the house perfectly. How do you think you will get away from the fortune that has fallen on you? If, being a mortal, you have more good things than bad, certainly you have done well.

But, dearest daughter, cease from unhappy thoughts, escape from an offence against the gods. For it is nothing if not that to wish to be stronger than the gods. Dare to love - a god wants it. Since you are ailing, turn the ailment into something good. There are charms and soothing spells. A drug will turn up for this complaint. You will wait a long time for a man to come up with a solution if we women do not find the way.

CHORUS   Phaidra, what she says is more practical for the present circumstances, though I commend you - but my approval may be more painful for you to hear than her words.

PHAIDRA   This is what destroys the well-governed cities and houses of men, words that are too fine. For you should not say things that will please, but how honour can be brought out of this.

NURSE   What solemn talk is this? You do not need becoming words but the man - won over as quickly as possible. Someone must speak to him and set him straight about your story. If this were not a matter of your life, if you were a self-disciplined woman, I would not egg you on for bed or pleasure. Now, however, the important thing is to save your life, and that is not hateful.

PHAIDRA   What a terrible thing you have said. Will you not shut your mouth and do not let out such shameful words again.

NURSE   Shameful, but better for you than noble words. Better to do it, if it saves you, than to die boasting of your good name.

PHAIDRA   By the gods, you speak well but of disgraceful things - go no farther. If you speak eloquently of shameful

57

things my good intentions will be overcome and I shall be overwhelmed by that from which I flee.

NURSE   If it seems right to you. You should not have sinned; as it is, be persuaded by me. For it is the second grace. I have in the house a magic potion, it has just come to my mind, which will end this ailment with no disgrace or harm to your mind - if you are not weak.

We need to take some sign from the desired one, a lock of hair, a piece of his clothes, then put them together and make one blessing from two.

PHAIDRA   Is this drug an ointment or a potion?

NURSE   I don't know. Benefit from it, don't look to learn, child.

PHAIDRA   I am afraid you may seem too clever for me.

NURSE   You are afraid of everything. What do you fear?

PHAIDRA   That you expose me to the son of Theseus.

NURSE   Let it go, daughter. I shall deal with these things well. Only be my companion in labour, Aphrodite, mistress of the sea. For the other things I am thinking of, it will suffice for me to speak with friends inside the house.

CHORUS   Eros, Eros, who sends desire that makes our eyes wet with tears, who brings sweet grace to the soul you set out to conquer, never appear to me with evil intent or undue measure! For neither fire nor the mighty weapon of the stars is like Aphrodite's arrow that comes from the hands of Eros, son of Zeus.

In vain by the River Alpheios or at the house of Phoibos Apollo at Delphi shall Hellas increase the killing of bulls, if we do not honour Eros, ruler of men, custodian of Aphrodite's chambers of love. When he comes, he destroys man's every circumstance.

Iole of Oichalia, an unyoked filly, a virgin and unwed, Aphrodite drove her like a restless Naiad, a Bacchant, from Eurytos, her father, with blood and smoke, for a deadly wedding, and gave her to Herakles, Alkmene's son. Oh, unhappy wedding!

Oh, holy wall of Thebes, Oh, mouth of Dirke, you both could tell what the coming of Aphrodite is like. With thunder and surrounding flame she brought to bed Semele, the mother of god-begotten Bacchos, a bride with a deathly fate. For her breath brings terror everywhere, and she flies hither and yon like a bee.

PHAIDRA   Be silent, women - I am ruined!

CHORUS   What terrible thing is happening in your house, Phaidra?

PHAIDRA   Hold back, I want to listen and find out everything that is going on inside.

CHORUS   I am silent. This is the prelude to something bad.

PHAIDRA   Oh, no! Please, no! My sufferings are worse!

CHORUS   What frightful things are you saying? What story are you shouting about? Tell me, lady, what word of violence threatens your heart?

PHAIDRA   I am destroyed. Stand by the door and listen to the kind of uproar that falls on the house.

CHORUS   You are by the keyhole, you should say what is coming from inside the house. Tell me, tell me whatever awful thing has happened.

PHAIDRA   The son of the horse-loving Amazon, Hippolytos, is shouting, saying terrible things to my servant.

CHORUS   I hear the sound, but not clearly. It came through the doors, the shouting came to you.

PHAIDRA   It is clear that he is bawling her out as a procuress, and traitor to her master's bed.

CHORUS   Oh, how dreadful. You are betrayed, dear one. What can I do to help you? For the hidden things have been revealed, and you will be destroyed because of it –

PHAIDRA   *(cries in despair)*

CHORUS   You are betrayed by a friend

PHAIDRA   She has destroyed me in telling my story, lovingly, hoping to make my illness better.

CHORUS   How then? What will you do, you who have not brought your sufferings upon yourself?

PHAIDRA   I know only one thing: I must die as quickly as possible, that is the only cure for the troubles I have now.

HIPPOLYTOS   Oh, Mother Earth! Oh, by the unclouded sun! What unspeakable words I have just heard!

NURSE   Be quiet, child, before someone hears you shouting!

HIPPOLYTOS   Having heard such awful things I am going to be quiet?

NURSE   Yes, by your fair right hand.

HIPPOLYTOS   Don't take my hand and don't touch my robe!

NURSE   I'm at your knees, don't shut me out completely.

HIPPOLYTOS   Why? If, as you say, you've done nothing wrong?

NURSE   This story, child, is not for common knowledge.

HIPPOLYTOS   It is better to speak of good things in front of lots of people.

NURSE   Child, you will surely not foreswear your oath?

HIPPOLYTOS   My tongue swore, my heart did not.

NURSE   Son, what will you do? Will you destroy those close to you?

HIPPOLYTOS   I have spit it out; no-one unrighteous is a friend to me.

NURSE   Forgive - human beings make mistakes, child.

HIPPOLYTOS   Oh, Zeus, why did you set down women, a deceitful evil to mankind, in the light of the sun? If you wanted to found a race of mortals, they ought not to be produced by women, better to place in your temples a weight of gold, or iron or bronze and buy the seedling sons, as appropriate to each man's income, then they could live in free homes without women. This is the proof that woman is a great evil: for the father who begot and raised her adds a dowry - she leaves home and he loses trouble. The one who takes this vile plant into his home is happy, covers her with adornments and clothes, beauty on ugliness, wretched man, dissipating the wealth of his house. It would be easier to marry a stupid woman, but she is useless in her simpleness. I hate a clever woman. A woman who thinks too much does not belong in my house. Aphrodite breeds more evil-doings in the clever ones. The one who cannot work things out avoids folly through the shortness of her wits. No servant should approach a woman, she should live surrounded by dumb and vicious beasts so that she could not talk to anyone or have anyone speak to her in return. As it is, those wicked ones inside the house have wicked plans, while their servants take them out in the outside world.

Just as you came, you vile piece of garbage, to procure me for my father's chaste bed. I'll purge away the things my ears have heard with flowing springs. How could I be so wicked, when I feel polluted just by hearing such things? Know this well, woman, my piety saves you. If I had not a taken an unbreakable oath before the gods, I would have told my father everything. Now I am leaving the house, because Theseus is out of the country. I shall keep quiet, but when I have come back with him I shall see how you and your mistress dare to look at him.

A bad end to you! I cannot speak enough of my hatred of women, not though they say I am always talking like this. But you are always wicked. Now whoever may teach them to control themselves can tell me not to trample on them.

PHAIDRA   What an unlucky destiny to be a woman. What craft do we have, when we have fallen, to break the hold of scandal? I get my just deserts. Oh, earth and light! Where can I escape fortune? How shall I hide this trouble, friends? What god could appear as my defender, which mortal could stand by me and be my colleague in unrighteous acts? This suffering

61

which has come upon my life in inescapable. I am the most unlucky of women.

CHORUS *(wails)* It is done, and the plans of your servant have not succeeded, mistress - you are in trouble.

PHAIDRA You worst of women, and destroyer of friends - see what you have done to me. Zeus, who gave me life, destroy you root and branch, blast you with fire! Did I not say - did I not foresee what you had in mind - to be silent about things by which I am now disgraced? You did not listen, and for that I am dying without honour. But I must make a new plan. That one, his mind sharpened by rage, will tell his father about me because of your wrong-doings, he will tell old Pittheus how things stand, he will fill the whole land with words of shame. May you perish, and any who think they know better than unwilling friends, and do not bring about a happy ending.

NURSE Mistress, you can blame me for my wrong-doings. The sting of your wound overcomes your judgement; but I have something to say about these things, if you will hear it. I brought you up and am your friend. Searching for a remedy for your illness I found one I did not intend. If I had succeeded, I would have been thought wise. For getting things right is a matter of luck.

PHAIDRA You think this is right and will satisfy me, to have wounded me and then bandy words with me?

NURSE We are talking too long. I was not wise. But there may still be a way to save you, child.

PHAIDRA Stop talking. You did not advise me well before and tried to do wicked things. Go away, and think about yourself. I shall order my affairs properly.

You, daughters of noble Troizenians, do me this favour, be silent and hide what you have heard here.

CHORUS I swear by holy Artemis, daughter of Zeus, never to bring to light your miseries.

PHAIDRA   You have spoken well. I have indeed found a remedy for the state I am in, a way to bequeath to my sons an honourable life, and myself to be helped in the face of what has now befallen. For I shall never shame the house of Crete, or face Theseus with shameful deeds, for the sake of one life.

CHORUS   What final dreadful thing do you intend to do?

PHAIDRA   To die - how, *I* shall decide.

CHORUS   Speak pure things!

PHAIDRA   And you give me good advice. I shall please Aphrodite, who has destroyed me, by losing my life today. I am defeated by ruthless love. But my dying will bring evil on another so that he will see not to be disdainful of my sufferings. He will share in my illness and learn moderation.

CHORUS   If only I could hide in earth's deepest hollows, God, make me a bird on the wing amongst feathered flocks; let me fly over the swell of the Adrian sea and the banks of the water of Eridanos. There the daughters of the sun let drop tears gleaming like amber into the purple sea, mourning for Phaëthon.

I would make my way to the bank planted with fruit-trees of the singing Hesperides, where the Lord of the Sea, of the purple shore, vouchsafes no road to sailors, reaching the sacred boundary of heaven which Atlas holds. Springs of ambrosia flow by the couches of Zeus's halls, where blessed earth increases most holy gifts of life for the gods.

Oh, white-winged Cretan ship which carried my lady across the roaring brine from her happy home to a most ill-fated marriage. For it boded ill both when you left Crete for renowned Athens and when they made fast the ends of the twisted cables and stepped onto the unknown shore of Athens' harbour at Mounichos.

There her heart was crushed by Aphrodite's terrible disease of unholy desire. Overwhelmed by a harsh turn of events, she will fasten a halter to the bridal chamber, fitting a noose around her white neck, with reverence for a hateful deity, choosing a glorious reputation and releasing her heart from the pain of love.

NURSE   *(From inside - the only stage direction in the Greek text)*

(cries out) Come and help, anyone nearby in the house! Our mistress, wife of Theseus, is strangling herself!

CHORUS   *(cries out)* It is done. The wife of the king is no more, hung in a noose.

NURSE   Why don't you hurry? Will someone not think of a two-edged blade so we can loosen the noose from her neck?

CHORUS   Friends, what shall we do? Should we go inside the house to loose the queen from the tight-drawn noose? Why? Are there not young manservants there? It is not safe in life to do too much.

NURSE   Set her straight, lay out her wretched body. This is a bitter housekeeping for my masters.

CHORUS   She is dead, the unhappy lady, so I hear. They are already laying out her corpse.

THESEUS   Women, do you know what that noise was inside the house? A grievous cry came from the servants. I am not greeted with joy and open doors when I return from the oracle. I hope nothing has happened to Pittheus? He is advanced in years, but all the same it would distress me if he had left the house.

CHORUS   The fortune that reaches out to you is not to do with old age, Theseus. The death of the young brings you pain.

THESEUS   Oh, no! The life of my children is not taken from me?

CHORUS   They live. The death of their mother is the worst pain for you.

THESEUS   What are you saying? She has died? How did this happen?

CHORUS   She made a noose with a rope and hanged herself.

THESEUS   Was she chilled with grief, or was there some other reason?

CHORUS   We know this much - for I too, Theseus, have just arrived at the house to mourn for your misfortunes.

THESEUS   Oh, no, no! Why did I set these twined leaves on my head, unhappy pilgrim that I am? *[He is wearing a laurel wreath denoting pilgrimage to the oracle]* Open the bars of the gates, servants, release the fastening, so that I can see the bitter spectacle of my wife, who destroys me in dying.

CHORUS   Oh, wretched in her miserable sufferings. You suffered, and worked such things as will confound this house. You are, you who die violently in unholy circumstances, a miserable triumph by your own hand. Poor woman, who darkens your life?

THESEUS   How I grieve. Oh, city, I have suffered the worst of my misfortunes. Fortune, how heavily you trample on me and on my house, an unspeakable blight from some avenger, a very destruction of life. Unhappy one, I look out over a sea of evils, so big that I can never sail back, nor pass through the flood of this circumstance. What wretched word, what grievous fate can I speak of, wife? For like some bird you have vanished from my hands, leaping eagerly from me to Hades. *(cries out)* These sufferings are terrible, terrible. I am caught up by some divine chance out of the past, by some sin committed long ago.

CHORUS   These evils have not come on you alone, Lord, many others share the loss of a dear wife.

THESEUS   I want the darkness below the earth, below the earth - to live in darkness, daring to die, with your dearest company taken from me. You destroyed more than your own perishing. Can I hear from someone? Where did it come from, poor wife, the deadly fortune for your heart? Someone tell me what happened, or does my royal house shelter a useless crowd of servants? What pain you give me. I have seen such terrible pain in my house, unendurable, unspeakable. I am destroyed, the house is empty, and the children are orphaned. You left those you bore, you left, dear one, the best of women who see the light of the sun or the radiance of the starry night.

CHORUS   Poor man, poor man. What misery your house has. My eyes flow with tears for your misfortunes; I tremble for the grief that is coming.

THESEUS   *(cries out)* But what is this tablet bound to her dear hand? Do you want to signal something new? Did the poor woman write letters, looking for some answers for our marriage, for the children? Have no fear, unhappy woman, for no other woman will enter the bed or house of Theseus. Now the impression of the seal of beaten gold of she who is no more greets me. Bring it, when I have unfolded the sealed coverings I shall see what the writing tablet wants to say to me.

CHORUS   Oh, no, no - a god brings a new evil to succeed the other. Another stroke of fortune makes life unliveable - let it happen. For I say that the house of our ruler is destroyed and no longer exists. Oh God, if it is possible, do not confound the house, I beg you to hear me. For like a seer I look on an omen.

THESEUS   No! This is evil upon evil, unbearable, not fit to read! I am accursed.

CHORUS   What is the matter? Tell me, if I may hear.

THESEUS   The tablet shouts, shouts insufferable things. Where can I flee the weight of evils? For I am ruined, destroyed. I have seen such things, endure such things the writing tells me.

CHORUS   *(cries out)* You are bringing to light the start of a story of misfortunes.

THESEUS   I can no longer contain this unbridled evil within the gate of my mouth. Oh, city! Hippolytos has dared to lay hands on my wife by force, dishonouring the eyes of holy Zeus. Father Poseidon, you once gave me three curses, make an end of my son with one of them - let him not escape this day, if those were true prayers for me!

CHORUS   Lord, ask that back, by the gods! You will know you are mistaken, believe me!

THESEUS   That is not possible. Furthermore, I exile him from this land. He will be struck by one of two fates, for either Poseidon will send him dying to the halls of Hades, respecting my prayers, or he will wander as an exile from this land and drain to the dregs his miserable life.

CHORUS   Here is your son, Hippolytos himself, just at the right time. Calm your dreadful anger, Lord Theseus, consider what is best for your house.

HIPPOLYTOS   I heard your cry, Father, and hurried here. I do not know what the matter is that causes you to lament, but I want to hear it from you. Oh! What's this? I see your wife, Father, dead. This is unbelievable, I just left her and she looked on the light as before.

What happened to her? By what turn of events did she die? Father, I want to hear about it from you. You are silent. Silence is no use in the midst of misfortunes. My heart longs to hear, and is eager to be a part of your troubles. It is not right for you to hide your ill-fortunes from friends, and those who are more than friends.

THESEUS   Oh, useless men who sin in so many ways, why do you teach ten thousand crafts, contrive everything, invent, but have not ordained or investigated one thing - to teach to think those who do not have a mind?

HIPPOLYTOS   He would be a remarkable teacher you are speaking of, who could compel those who do not think to reason. But you are not telling a very suitable tale, Father. I fear that grief is making you talk wildly.

THESEUS   There should be a touchstone for mortals, so that one could see clearly what lies in the hearts of those who are near, to know who is true and who is no friend; all men should have two voices, one righteous, the other what it actually is, so that the unjust one would be convicted by the just one, and we should not be cheated.

HIPPOLYTOS   Has one of our friends slandered me, who am infected although blameless? I am thunderstruck. You strike out at me saying things that are mad, senseless.

THESEUS   The heart of man - how far will it go? What will be the limit to audacity and insolence? For if it increases in every generation, the next one will surpass the last in villainy, the gods will need to produce another earth, which will make room for the unjust and evil-natured.

Look at this one, who is my own son and shamed my bed, who is clearly convicted as the worst of men by the dead woman. Show yourself here to your father's face, although you are polluted. You, then, are the extraordinary man who associates with the gods? You are the sensible one and undefiled by evils? I would not be persuaded by your boasts - you in your perverse thinking charge the gods with ignorance. Now boast about your cultish food without a soul, adore your lord Orpheus, honour him with verbose vapourings! You've been caught. I say to you all, flee from men like this. They use exalted words while doing shameful deeds. She is dead. Do you think that will save you? You are all the more entrapped by it, you scum. What oaths, what words could be stronger than hers, so that you could escape blame? You say she hated you, and enmity is natural between the bastard and the freeborn. You say she was a poor trafficker in life if she lost the dearest thing she had out of hostility to you? Are men without folly and women prone to it? I know young men are no more steadfast than women when Aphrodite disturbs the youthful - that, in itself, rises up to help them. Now then, why should I bandy words with you, when this dead body is the clearest witness? Flee into exile from this land as quickly as possible, never enter the god-built walls of Athens or the boundaries of any land where my sceptre rules. If I weakly accept what I suffer at your hands, Sinis the Isthmian will not bear witness that I killed him but that it is vain boasting, nor will the rocks of Skiron, which lie between two seas, say that I weigh heavily upon evil men.

CHORUS   I do not know how I could say any mortal is lucky. For what existed before is overturned.

HIPPOLYTOS   Father, the passion and commitment of your heart are terrible. Although these words appear to be fair if, however, one examines them, they are not. I am unskilled in public speaking, clearer amongst my peers and small numbers. This is natural. Those who appear foolish among the wise seem more inspired to the crowd. All the same I must, given what has happened, let loose my tongue. I shall begin first of all by speaking to the matter with which you first set a trap for me to throw me and leave me unable to answer. You see this light and the earth, in them there is no man, deny it as you will, who is more self-disciplined than I am. For I know, first of all, to revere the gods, to have friends who practice no injustice, who would be ashamed to proclaim wickedness or return a kindness with shameful things. Nor have I mocked those with whom I associate, Father, but am the same to my friends present or absent. Secondly, I am untouched by that in which you think you have caught me. My body is to this day pure of sex. I know nothing of the act but words I have heard or pictures I have seen. Nor am I keen to look at such things, for I have a virgin soul. Yet my continence does not convince you. Well then, you must show by what means I was corrupted. Was this woman's body the most beautiful of all women's? Or did I hope to take over your house by a profitable marriage? I would be a fool and not in my right mind. Just how pleasant is it to rule? Anything but to the wise - kingship destroys the minds of those mortals whom it pleases. What I want is to win in the Hellenic Games, but come second in city life, always fortunate with the

69

best people as my friends. So I have freedom of action and being without danger offers a greater blessing than rule.

You have heard everything except for one thing, if I had a witness like myself, or if she were alive to be at my trial, on investigating the events you would see the guilty. Now I swear to you an oath by Zeus and the land's plain, I never touched your wife, nor wished to, nor had it in mind. May I die dishonoured, unknown, without city or home, an exile wandering over the earth, if I am a wicked man. I do not know if she lost her life through fear. It is not right for me to say any more. She behaved with continence, not being continent; I have it but have not done well out of it.

CHORUS   What you have said must clear you from blame. You have provided holy oaths, which are persuasive.

THESEUS   Is this man not a charmer and a sorcerer, who tried to overcome my heart with his smooth temper, after shaming his father?

HIPPOLYTOS   It is your own that I really wonder at, Father, for if you were the son and I your father, I would not have punished you with exile, if you had thought fit to touch my wife.

THESEUS   You say just the right thing. You shall not die that way. For a quick death is easiest for a scoundrel. But you will go wandering from your native land, according to the law you have laid down for yourself - you will drain your miserable life to the dregs on alien earth. This is the reward for an impious man.

HIPPOLYTOS   No, what will you do? Will you not allow time to bring to light the truth about me, but exile me from this land?

THESEUS   Beyond the Black Sea and the bounds of the Atlantic, if I can, I hate the sight of you so much.

HIPPOLYTOS   You will accept no oath or pledge or words of a seer, but throw me out of the land unjudged?

THESEUS   The tablet convicts you convincingly, even if it is not an oracle. The birds of ill-omen that fly overhead - good riddance to them.

HIPPOLYTOS   Gods, why do I not release my mouth? I am being destroyed because of you, whom I revere. No. I would not be believed in any way about the things I need to be. I would violate the oath I swore in vain.

THESEUS   This piety of yours kills me. Are you not leaving your native land as quickly as possible?

HIPPOLYTOS   Where can I go in such a wretched state? Which friend's house can I enter, fleeing such a charge?

THESEUS   Whoever delights in providing for defilers of women as guests and companions of evil.

HIPPOLYTOS   You gut me. Tears are near if I appear to be wicked, and seem so to you too.

THESEUS   You should have groaned then and thought what you were doing when you dared to commit an outrage on your father's wife.

HIPPOLYTOS   Oh, house - if you had a voice and could speak for me, and bear witness if I am a wicked man!

THESEUS   You do wisely in appealing to dumb witnesses. Saying that reveals you as wicked.

HIPPOLYTOS   Oh - if only I could stand apart from myself and look myself in the face, so that I could weep for the evils that I have suffered.

THESEUS   You are far more practised in self-worship than acting justly to your father.

HIPPOLYTOS   My unhappy mother, what a bitter birth! May none of those dear to me be a bastard.

THESEUS   Why don't you drag him away, slaves? Did you not hear long ago that I pronounced him banished?

HIPPOLYTOS   It will be the worse for any of them that touches me. You yourself, if that is what you want, throw me out of the house.

THESEUS   I shall do that, if you do not obey my words. No pity for your exile wins me over.

HIPPOLYTOS   It is settled, so it seems. I am in misery. I know things, but I do not know how to say them. *[Probably addresses statue of Artemis]* Oh, dearest of the gods to me, daughter of Leto, my partner, my companion in the hunt, I am banished from renowned Athens. Farewell, city and land of Erechtheus. Oh, plain of Troizen, how happy a place to grow up in, farewell. Looking at you I make my last statement.

Come, young men, my companions in this land, say farewell and escort me from this country. You will never see a more wise and prudent man than me, even if it does not seem like that to my father.

[The chorus may be huntsmen for at least two of the sections of the following choral passage - there is linguistic evidence for masculine speakers. It is very unexpected to change chorus and how one section or all would get out of the orchestra, change costume, or more likely just mask, and get back on again is a big question, especially as the chorus is supposed to come on and stay on throughout, but it might make for interesting dramatic interpretation. A chorus divided in parts and singing antiphonally is quite normal, as is the likelihood of a leader or spokesman/woman for dialogue with the actors, but this short section is definitely problematic in having two possible identities for the chorus and hence some translators leave it out. I have indicated where the huntsmen may be speaking - it is up to director and cast to decide what will work/is feasible on stage at this point.]

CHORUS *[?Hunstmen]*   When it comes to my mind how great the care of the gods is for men, it relieves my sorrow. Though hope is hidden deep it leaves me when I look on the

72

fortunes and deeds of men. For one change comes out of another, and from this the life of man is endless wanderings.

[?Troizenian Women] Heaven hear my prayer and fate grant me this good fortune and a life untouched by pain. May my thoughts be neither dogmatic nor false. May my life always share in good fortune, an easy character changing for tomorrow.

[?Huntsmen] I no longer have a clear mind, looking for hope, when we see, we see the brightest star of Greek Athens going to another land because of his father's rage. Oh, sands on my country's shore, oh, mountain thicket where with holy Diktynna he killed after the hunt with swift hounds.

[?] No longer will you leap up behind your yoked horses, holding your course around the shore with the foot of a trained horse. The sleepless music from the bridge of the lyre will be silent in your father's house. The resting places of the daughter of Leto in the deep spring grass will be without garlands. You have killed by your exile the struggle of the maidens who hoped to win your love.

I myself shall draw out with tears a lifeless life. Unhappy mother, you had little good from the birth of your son. Oh, I am angry with the gods! Sister Graces, why do you send the poor man, who is not to blame, from his native land, from his home?

I see an attendant of Hippolytos running, sad-faced, to the house.

MESSENGER   Where can I find Lord Theseus, women? If you know, show me. Is he in the palace?
CHORUS   Here he is, he is coming out of the house.

MESSENGER   Theseus, I bring you word of weighty concern for you, and for the citizens who live in the city of Athens or within the bounds of the lands of Troizen.

THESEUS   What is it? Has something new or worse fallen upon the neighbouring cities?

MESSENGER   Hippolytos is no more - or almost. He still sees the light, but his life is in the balance.

THESEUS   By whose hand? Did someone become his enemy because he had taken his wife by force as he did his father's?

MESSENGER   His own chariot killed him, and the curse out of your own mouth, which you called down on your son from your father, the ruler of the sea.

THESEUS   Oh, gods, and Poseidon! You must be truly my father, having heard my entreaties. How was he destroyed? Tell me. In what way did Justice spring her trap on the one who shamed me?

MESSENGER   We were weeping where the shore meets the waves, grooming the horses, combing their manes. For a messenger came saying that Hippolytos could no longer set foot in the land, having to endure exile because of you. He himself came to us on the shore with a sad song. A throng of young men was with him, many followers and friends. After a time, when he had stopped groaning, he said, "Why am I so distracted? I must obey my father's words. Harness my horses, slaves, and yoke them to the chariot - for this is no longer my city."

Then each man got to work, and quicker than you could say it, they were harnessed and set up by our master himself. He caught the reins in his hand from the rail, his feet were fastened with shoes. First he held up his hands to the gods, "Zeus, may I die if I am an evil man. May my father learn, whether I live or die, how he dishonours me."

74

Then he took the goad in his hand and urged on the team. We servants were accompanying our master, hard by the reins, on the direct road to Argos and Epidauria.

When we had come to the empty countryside beyond this land where a headland lies facing what is already the Saronic Gulf, there a noise came from the earth, like the thunder of Zeus, a deep rumbling, horrible to hear. The horses held their heads high and pricked their ears to heaven. Amongst us there was a fresh panic, wondering where the noise came from. Looking out to the sea-beaten shore we saw an unearthly wave reaching to heaven so that it prevented my eyes from seeing Skiron's shores. It hid the Isthmus and Asklepios' rock. Then, swelling up, foaming and frothing all around, it came to the shore from the swollen sea, towards the four-horse chariot. At the moment the triple surge of the wave broke it threw out a bull, a fearsome monster. Its bellowing filled the whole earth with a terrifying re-echo - we were watching, but it was too dreadful to behold. Immediately a terrible fear fell on the horses. Our master, well-versed and at home with the ways of horses, took the reins in his hands, he dragged on them, leaning back like a sailor on the oar. The horses champed down on the wrought-iron bits in their mouths and bore on forcibly, nor were they turned by the steersman's hand, nor the reins, nor the close-jointed chariot. When he tried to steer their course to the stoneless land the bull appeared in front of them, so that it turned them back, the four-horse team going mad with fright. If their madness was carrying them towards the rocks it kept close by the rail, in silence, to the moment when it rose up and overturned them, forcing the wheel onto a rock. Everything was confusion - the wheels, hubs, axles, lynch-pins. The poor man, tangled in the reins, inextricably bound, was dragged along. His dear head was dashed on the rock, his flesh ripped, his cries were terrible to hear. "Stop! You were reared in my stables, don't destroy me! Oh, Father - your wretched curse. Who is here to help the best of men?"

Many were willing, but we were left far behind. Then, released from the cutwork reins - I don't know how - he fell, still breathing, but life would be short. The horses had disappeared and I could not see that terrible monster of a bull anywhere on the rocky land.

I am a slave of your house, Lord, but I shall never be persuaded your son is so wicked, not if the whole race of women were to hang themselves and filled every pine on Mount Ida with letters. I know him to be noble.

CHORUS   *(wails)* New evils are accomplished - it is not possible to escape the fate that must be.

THESEUS   Because of my hate for the man who has suffered these things your words at first pleased me, but now out of respect for the gods and because he is my son, I am neither pleased nor suffer at his misfortunes.

MESSENGER   What then? Should we bring the poor wretch here - would that find favour with you? Think - use my advice, don't be cruel to your son while he is suffering.

THESEUS   Bring him, so that, seeing with my eyes the man who denies he dishonoured my bed, I can condemn him with words and the co-operation of the gods.

CHORUS   You, Aphrodite, lead captive the stubborn hearts of gods and mortals, and with you, the one with colourful wings and the swiftest flight besets them. He hovers between the tuneful earth and the salt sea. Winged Eros, gleaming with gold, charms and assails with madness of the heart young beasts of the mountains and of the sea, all which the earth nurtures. He charms whatever beholds the sun, and men too. You alone reign in queenly honour over everything, Aphrodite.

ARTEMIS   I order you, nobly born son of Aigeus, listen! Artemis, daughter of Leto, speaks to you. Theseus, wretched man, why do you take pleasure in these things? You have killed your son, which is unholy. You believed the lying stories of your wife without proof. You will have a public ruin. Will you not hide in shame in Tartaros beneath the earth, or change into a bird to fly away from this evil? You can have no share in the life of good men.

Listen, Theseus, to the state of your wretchedness. I shall not smooth anything over, I shall hurt you. But this is what I came for, to show your son's righteous heart, so that he may die with a good name, and also your wife's mad passion and, in a way, her nobility. For she was stung, by the most hateful of the gods to me, and all those who take pleasure in virginity, with passion for your son. While she was trying to defeat Aphrodite by will-power, plans she did not want brought her to destruction, when a woman explained her ailment to your son, under oath. He, because he is an upright man, did not yield to her words nor, when he was being wronged by you, did he break his oath, showing his reverence. She then, in fear that she might be found out, wrote the letter and destroyed your son with guile. But you believed it all the same.

THESEUS   No!

ARTEMIS   Does my story sting you, Theseus? Keep quiet, because you have things to hear that will make you suffer more. You know those three sure curses you have from your father? You have misused one, you worst of men, against your own son, when you could have used it against an enemy. Your father from the sea gave it to you willingly, as he should - he had promised. But you, you are shown wicked to him and to me because you waited for no pledge or oracular proof, you made no examination or provided time for slow perusal. You thought it better to curse quickly, and killed your son.

THESEUS   Mistress, let me die.

ARTEMIS   You have done terrible things, but still it is possible for you to find forgiveness. For Aphrodite willed these things to happen, satisfying her anger. The gods have this law -

none gets in the way of another's wishes, but always lets it be. But know this well, if I did not fear Zeus, I would not have come to this shame that I could let the man who is dearest of all mortals to me die. As for your son, first, the fact that you did not know acquits you of evil, then, in dying your wife prevented an investigation so that you were forced to believe her. Now these evils have broken mostly upon you, but I too grieve. It does not please the gods when the reverent die. Those who are wicked, we destroy them with their children and their houses.

CHORUS   The poor man is coming now, his young flesh and his golden hair spoiled. Oh, troubled house, encompassed by a double grief from the gods.

HIPPOLYTOS   *(cries out)* Pity me, mistreated by the unjust words of an unjust father. I am dying in misery. My head is pierced with pain and my brain leaping in spasms. Hold me, I am failing, I must rest. Hateful chariot team, fed by my own hand, you have destroyed me utterly, done me to death. *(cries out)* By the gods, slaves, touch my wounded body gently! Who stands at my right side? Lift me carefully, carry me straight, god-forsaken and cursed by my father's fault. Zeus, Zeus, do you see these things? I, who was holy and reverent, who excelled all in modesty, I go seeing Hades before me, I have utterly lost my life. I worked labours of piety towards men for no purpose.

(cries out) Now pain, pain comes upon me! Let me go, damn you! Let the healer, death, help me. Kill me, kill me, the accursed one. I am desperate for a two-edged sword to rend myself asunder, lay my life to rest. Oh, terrible curse of my father, this evil come forth from the blood-guilt of ancient ancestors, and it does not wait, it falls on me - but why, when I have done nothing wrong? *(cries out)* What can I say? How can I release my life from unfeeling suffering? If only I could lay myself down in the black night of Lord Hades.

78

ARTEMIS   Poor man, yoked to such a fate. Your nobility of heart has killed you.

HIPPOLYTOS   Oh, breath of divine fragrance. Even in my misery my body is eased by hearing you. The goddess Artemis is in this place.

ARTEMIS   She is, unhappy man, dearest to you of all the gods.

HIPPOLYTOS   Do you see how things are with me, Mistress, how pitiful?

ARTEMIS   I see, but it is not right for tears to come from my eyes.

HIPPOLYTOS   You have no hunter, no servant –

ARTEMIS   No indeed. You are very dear to me, even in death.

HIPPOLYTOS   - nor keeper of your houses, nor guardian of your statues.

ARTEMIS   It was the deceitful Aphrodite who devised it all.

HIPPOLYTOS   Oh - now I know the god who has destroyed me.

ARTEMIS   She resented your neglect and hated your continence.

HIPPOLYTOS   I understand. Aphrodite has destroyed three of us.

ARTEMIS   Your father and you and his wife the third.

HIPPOLYTOS   I mourn for my father's ill-fortune.

ARTEMIS   You were deceived by the plans of a god.

HIPPOLYTOS   What terrible things have happened to you, Father.

THESEUS   I wish I could die, child. There is nothing to please me in life.

HIPPOLYTOS   I grieve for you more than me, for your wrong-doing.

THESEUS   If only I could become a corpse instead of you, child.

HIPPOLYTOS   What bitter gifts from your father, Poseidon.

THESEUS   If only that prayer had never come to my lips.

HIPPOLYTOS   What then? You would have killed me, because you were so angry.

THESEUS   My wits were confused by the gods.

HIPPOLYTOS   I wish the race of men could curse the gods.

ARTEMIS   Let it be. For in the darkness under the earth you will not be unavenged for the things that fell upon your body out of the angry intentions of Aphrodite because of your reverence and good heart. I shall take vengeance with my own hand on whatever mortal is dearest to her, with these inescapable arrows. Poor man, in return for your sufferings I shall give you very great honours in the city of Troizen. Unmarried girls will cut their hair for you before their weddings, you shall reap a great harvest of grief and tears throughout the ages. Girls will always have skill in singing of you, and Phaidra's love will have a name and not be held in silence.

You, son of old Aigeus, take your son in your arms and hold him close, for you killed him unwillingly. It is reasonable for men to do wrong when the gods ordain it. I bid you not to hate your father, Hippolytos. You have a fate by which you are destroyed.

Now, farewell. It is not right for me to look upon the dead, nor to pollute my eyes with the last breath of the dying. I see that evil is already near you.

HIPPOLYTOS   Go rejoicing, happy virgin. You leave our long companionship easily. As you desire, I release blame from my father, for I obeyed your words in the past.

(cries out) Darkness comes to my eyes. Take hold of me father, set my body straight.

THESEUS   Oh, child, what are you doing to me, accursed as I am?

HIPPOLYTOS   I am dying, and see the gates of the underworld.

THESEUS   Will you leave me with an impure hand?

HIPPOLYTOS   No - I absolve you of murder.

THESEUS   What are you saying? You release me from blood-guilt?

HIPPOLYTOS   I call to witness Artemis of the conquering bow.

THESEUS   Dearest son, how noble you seem to your father.

HIPPOLYTOS   Pray that happens with your legitimate children.

THESEUS   A reverent and noble heart!

HIPPOLYTOS   Goodbye, many goodbyes from me, Father.

THESEUS   Don't abandon me, child - be strong.

HIPPOLYTOS   I have finished being strong. I am dying, Father. Hide my face in my robes quickly.

THESEUS   Oh, boundaries of renowned Athens, city of Pallas, such a man has been taken from you. I am in misery. How many times, Aphrodite, I shall remember your evil-doings.

CHORUS   This pain, common to all citizens, came unexpectedly. There will be a downpour of many tears. The fame of the great endures, commanding greater sorrow.

GUIDE TO NAMES AND PLACES

With both Transliterated and Latinised Versions

Adrian Sea The Adriatic
Alpheios (*Alphaeus*) The river that runs by Olympia
Amazon A race of warrior women in Asia Minor
Aphrodite Goddess of sex and love, forces without which there is no life
Apollo God of prophecy, healing, light, brother to Artemis
Argos (*Argus*) Major city of the Argolid (North-East Peloponnese)
Ariadne Sister of Phaidra. When Theseus came to Crete as part of the Athenian tribute to Minos (7 youths and 7 maidens to be offered to the Minotaur), she fell in love with him and helped him to slay the Minotaur and escape the Labyrinth in which he had lived. By way of thanks, Theseus dumped her on the island of Naxos, but there Dionysos (god of wine and wild nature) found her and became her lover
Artemis Goddess of the hunt, a virgin goddess who also aids women in childbirth
Asklepios' Rock Asklepios (*Aesculapius*), the healing god, is associated with Epidauros, where a major healing sanctuary was built in his honour
Atlantic Gates The Straits of Gibraltar
Atlas A Titan, he holds the earth on his shoulders. He is to be found in the far West
Bacchos (*Bacchus*) Another name for Dionysos
Cyprian Aphrodite was born of the sea-foam off the island of Cyprus, and can be referred to by mentioning the island

Demeter   Goddess of grain and fertility. Unusual in that fasting can be part of her rites - not a normal discipline in the Greek world. The focus of various mystery cults (particularly the Eleusinian Mysteries, celebrated for her and her daughter Persephone) and mystery elements in other cults

Diktynna (*Dictynna*)   A Cretan goddess, possibly to be identified with Artemis (*dictys* = hunting net)

Dirke (*Dirce*)   Wife of Lykos, King of Thebes. She treated her niece-by-marriage, Antiope, so cruelly that Antiope's sons tied her to a rampaging bull. The spring is supposedly where it finally threw her remains off

Epidauria   Area round **Epidauros** (North-East Peloponnese)

Erechtheus   Legendary early king of Athens

Eridanos   A mythical river, but thought to be in the North

Eros   The child of Aphrodite whose arrows impose love from without

Euxine   The Black Sea

The Garden of the Hesperides   Mythical garden in the far West where the golden apples grow. Fetching them was one of Herakles' labours.

The Graces   Nymphs with no clear mythological role, can be seen as attendants on Aphrodite

Hekate (*Hecate*)   An underworld (chthonic) goddess particularly associated with witches

Hellas   Greece

Hippolytos (*Hippolytus*)   Son of Theseus and the Amazon **Hippolyta** - versions vary on how willing she was about this.

Iole   Offered as a prize in an archery contest by her father, Eurytos (*Eurytus*), who did not expect to lose. He was beaten by Herakles (*Hercules*), who later killed Eurytos and took Iole as his concubine. It was in despair over this that Deïaneira persuaded him to wear the cloak soaked in the blood of the centaur Nessos that she thought was a love charm, but which was actually deadly

Kephalos (*Cephalus*) Grandson of Erechtheus, son of the messenger god Hermes. The goddess of Dawn (**Eos**) fell for him and snatched him up to heaven

Kybele (*Cybele*) The Great Mother of Asia Minor, an ancient goddess. Her rites include ecstatic worship

Leto A Titaness (an earlier generation of divinities, ousted by the Olympian Gods), mother of Artemis and Apollo by Zeus

Mounichos (*Munychia*) Referring to one of Athens' harbours

Mysteries Refers here to the Eleusinian Mysteries, to which anyone could be initiated - which made it unusual for Greek society- but all initiates must follow certain rites and processes in Athens before full participation in the revelation of the Mysteries at Eleusis (14 miles from Athens)

Oichalia (*Oechalia*) It is unclear where this city was meant to be, locations as diverse as Messenia, Euboia (*Euboea*) and Thessaly were suggested in ancient times

Orpheus The gifted musician who nearly rescued his dead wife, Eurydike (*Eurydice*), from Hades. He ended his days torn to pieces by maddened women, but became the centre of an ecstatic mystery cult himself

Pallantides A family opposed to Aigeus (*Aegeus*), killed by Theseus. He is spending time in exile in Troizen in expiation of this

Pallas An epithet of Athene

Pan Nature god who can be sensed, not always benignly, in wild places (hence panic)

Pandion Legendary early king of Athens

Pasiphaë Mother of Phaidra. When Minos offended Poseidon, the god made Pasiphaë fall in love with a bull (his creature). The product of this union was the Minotaur

Pelops The hero from whom the Peloponnese derives its name - although his heroic acts included cheating and murder

Phaëthon Son of the Sun-God, he asked to be allowed to drive the sun-chariot, which of course he could not control, and he crashed and fell into the Eridanos (*Eridanus*). His sisters wept for him and were changed into poplar trees and thereafter their tears became amber

Phaidra (*Phaedra*) Wife of Theseus, daughter of Minos of Crete and Pasiphaë, sister of Ariadne and half-sister of the Minotaur

Pittheus King of Troizen (*Troezen*), he has various connections with Aigeus, Theseus and Hippolyta. Hippolytos has been brought up in his household (having sons brought up and trained in other households is a normal Heroic process, cf. knights and squires in England)

Poseidon God of the sea and here father to Theseus (the Greeks were not troubled by the idea of legendary characters having both a divine and a human father to be named and called on depending on circumstances - this is not the only example), to whom he has given three curses

Pythian To do with Delphi, the greatest of all Greek oracle sites and considered to be the centre of the world. Associated with Apollo

Semele Human mother of Dionysos by Zeus. She asked to see Zeus in his full divine glory (mistake) and was burnt to a crisp. She did get deified afterwards, however, under the name Thyone

Sinis Nasty piece of work who lived on the Isthmus of Corinth and tied those who fell into his path to bent pine trees (which he then unbent ...). Killed by Theseus

Skiron (*Sciron*) Nasty piece of work who lived on the Isthmus of Corinth and kicked his victims into the sea, where they were eaten by a monstrous sea turtle. Killed by Theseus

Thebes Major city in Boiotia (*Boeotia*), North of Attika (*Attica*). Memorable legendary Thebans include the family of Oidipous (*Oedipus*)

Theseus Hero and King of Athens. His adventures include ridding the Isthmus of Corinth of assorted villains and slaying the Minotaur. His human father is Aigeus, but in this play he is also the son of Poseidon (*q.v.*)

Thessaly Region of North-East Greece noted for horse-rearing and witches

Troizen (*Troezen*)   A city on the East coast of the Peloponnese, across the Saronic Gulf from Attika

Zeus King of the gods, worshipped in many aspects. He has a very over-active libido and satisfies it in taking some unexpected forms e.g. swan, shower of gold ... One of his important functions is the oversight of oaths, which are sacred to the Greek world